The McClure Collection

given by
J. WARREN and LOIS McCLURE

in support of the
RIT College of Business

Wallace Memorial Library
Rochester Institute of Technology

Aspen's Nonprofit Management Series

Effective Nonprofit Management

Essential Lessons for Executive Directors

Aspen's Nonprofit Management Series

Extraordinary Board Leadership:
The Seven Keys to High-Impact Governance

Doug Eadie

Effective Nonprofit Management:
Essential Lessons for Executive Directors

Robert L. Lewis

Nonprofit Mergers: The Power of Successful Partnerships

Dan H. McCormick

Aspen's Nonprofit Management Series

Effective Nonprofit Management

Essential Lessons for Executive Directors

Robert L. Lewis, LLB, JD
Director
Trusteeship Initiative
Mandel Center for Nonprofit Organizations
of Case Western Resesrve University
Professor of Governance
School of Law
Case Western Reserve University
Cleveland, Ohio

AN ASPEN PUBLICATION®
Aspen Publishers, Inc.
Gaithersburg, Maryland
2001

Library of Congress Cataloging-in-Publication Data available upon request.

Orders: (800) 638-8437
Customer Service: (800) 234-1660

Editorial Services: Timothy Sniffin
ISBN: 0-8342-2056-3

Printed in the United States of America

1 2 3 4 5

Dedication

If nothing else, this book has taught me how to use a computer. It was a sometimes angry struggle, but I persevered in dedication to:

- My five grown children—Dr. Brian, Dr. Paul, David, Pavia, and Clea—each of whom has dedicated him- or herself to teaching, healing, culture, and beauty in one form or another, and each of whom has a stable spousal or equivalent relationship.

- My seven grandchildren: Zachary, Jordan, Lea Yi, Lewie, Delphine, Madeline, and Xiou Xiou.

- That woman known in the text as Joanne, who took the challenge of marrying a widower with three sons, adding two daughters of our own to the roster (11 months apart); nursed and nagged me back to health after two heart surgeries; is herself a historian and published author; lived with the gypsies in the caves of Spain; refers to herself as a prehistoric hippie; and inspired me to activities beyond my years and capabilities.

Table of Contents

Foreword

To be asked by Robert Lewis to write these words is a high honor, for if there is anyone alive with more wisdom about, and experience in, the nonprofit world, that person has not come my way. Moreover, for more than a half century, Lewis has generously applied his governance genius to hundreds of organizations and has managed to do so monogamously. Some years ago, a group of self-important bankers published a "manifesto" purporting to be some sort of edict or operating manual for those who sit concurrently on boards of several colleges. Robert took instant umbrage, firing off a blistering letter that emphasized the duty of loyalty and the impossibility of being truly loyal to more than one institution at a time. Reading this, I became suddenly aware of my own trashy ways and took immediate steps to recover my purity.

Do not be deceived by the smallness of this book; its advice has large implications. If its lessons could somehow be applied to all of our nation's nonprofits, there would ensue a blinding flash of clarity that would in turn cause a marked improvement in the effectiveness of the delivery of the services that each mission of these agencies promises.

Indeed, *mission* is our starting point: What do we do and for whom do we do it? Not why, not how. Sadly (actually hilariously), the garish, bloated prose of the mission statements of both nonprofits and for-profits richly lends itself to satire. *Good Companies Don't Have Mission Statements,* by Digby Anderson of the United Kingdom, sends up such statements merely by quoting them, easy targets as they are, bringing tears of laughter to his readers' eyes. BP Amoco, for example, claims that "we are a force for good in all that we do," causing the author to wonder whether this oil company has mistaken itself for God. Given the degree of overinflation in the mission statements of hard-headed, bottom-line multinational corporations, just imagine some of the high-flying absurdities captured in such statements of idealistic nonprofits! Such fluff and frippery serve only to encourage Dilbert-esque jokes, even cynicism. So keep it simple, Lewis says. Avoid adjectives. Save poetry for more suitable settings.

In nonprofits, the poetry is not in the writing, but in the doing. Zeal and commitment are essential ingredients of good executive directors and trustees alike. Yet, as John Gardner reminds us, in this sacred arena, there is no worse combination than passion and incompetence.

Let us return to Robert Lewis, *mensch* yet honorary Greek, *anax adron,* leader of men (yet followed more often by women), wise counselor, direct descendant of Mentor the original, trusted advisor to Telemachus in the *Odyssey*, yet metamorphosing now into Nestor, the oldest and wisest warrior of the Trojan War, with advice given in admitted semi-curmudgeonly fashion, less gently than in earlier days. So much good counsel to dispense, so little time to give it.

Metaphorically, Robert is a fine old wine that maketh glad the heart of man. And women. And is not old wine the best? At midlife, Disraeli claimed to prefer bad wine to good: "One gets so bored with good wine." One cannot become bored with Robert Lewis. Still, in this book, the wine has become a soupcon less smooth to the palate. Certainly not the Mexican peasant "wine of the three shivers," yet with a distinct bite, almost an essence of vinegar as though it is preparing to turn. But do not be fooled by the apparent change in this fermented grape, nor by its clever new-bottle disguise. For within this gruff-talking, pugnacious guide to nonprofit leadership still resides our friend of manners gentle, of affection mild—in wit a man, simplicity a child. With childlike mien, this intellectual giant has helped countless hundreds of organizations, trustees, executive directors, and others in their, and his, pursuit of service to humankind.

In so doing, Lewis has fulfilled as well his own mission as a human being. An older friend, much older than Robert, once revealed to me the purpose of his life, our mission here on earth. It is, he said simply, to entertain the angels. Robert Lewis continues to do this, and to entertain others as well. After all, why not? He started in vaudeville.

Unlike earthbound beings, angels of every order have millions of channels from which to choose. So whenever one hears a celestial click, one should recognize that they have lost interest and moved on.

This is what I must do. And although I am flattered beyond description to have had this honor, I would still prefer to have had the last word, rather than the first ones.

—Thomas R. Horton
Former Vice President of Marketing
IBM Corporation
Armonk, New York
Former Chairman
Association of Governing Boards of Universities and Colleges
Washington, DC
Co-founder
National Center for Nonprofit Boards
Washington, DC
Former Chairman
National Association of Corporate Directors
Washington, DC

Introduction

As an executive director of a nonprofit agency (I'll call you the "ED" from here on), you live your professional life with and under the aegis of a disparate group of people known as the board of trustees. That relationship can run the gamut from being gratifying to being horrifying, depending on a lot of things that enter into the human equation. If the problems become too numerous or complicated, the situation can spill over even into your private life. The purpose of this little book is to set forth some ideas that will be helpful in avoiding some of the problems that I see repeating themselves as I do my consulting with nonprofit boards and their EDs. Where grammatical purity allows, I have put the title of each lesson in the form of a rule for you to follow. For some titles, I have had to improvise.

I present these ideas in a simple and straightforward way. Just basic, hard-hitting thoughts and suggestions that have been tested in the field—and that *work*. And if you want fuller explanations or want to argue about something, feel free to communicate with me at my home in Cleveland Heights, Ohio. My e-mail address is rojolewis@aol.com. Somewhere in this work, you'll be stumbling on some autobiographical stuff, so you'll know something about my diverse career moves.

If I seem brusque at times, attribute that to the impatience of an octogenarian who still thinks that he has a lot worthwhile to say and an ever-diminishing time in which to say it. Well, I do have a lot to say about the subject at hand. I come from a background of trusteeship, I've been immersed in it for more years than I care to say, and I consider it a sacred concept. Without your help, your board may never realize that. So a lot of what I'm telling you may have to be repackaged in a form appropriate for you, in turn, to tell *them*. It's ironic that *you*, being professionally subordinate to your trustees, may have to advise and instruct *them—your supposed superiors*—how to act as a board. But that's the way it is most of the time.

My chief motivations (there are two) in writing this work are to explode some myths that surround nonprofit leadership. One that particularly infuriates me is that the relationship between you and your board is akin to that of a marriage or a partnership, and that it's all soft and warm and furry and semi-saintly. You'll be invited to a lot of workshops and seminars and professional meetings where some Pollyana-ish, supposed expert in the nonprofit field will be spouting that rubbish. Well, that sentiment, in addition to having its outrightly disgusting aspects (how would you like to be married to *your* board chair?), is neither an accurate nor a desirable description of what life is like for you in your job as ED. So we're going to face the realities.

First, a bit of basic terminology. You are that part of the sector of the nonprofit organization known as its "leadership." This sector, in turn, is divided into two smaller parts:

1. the "governance" component, composed of its board of trustees, with *its* particular jurisdiction and accountability in the life of the agency

2. the "management" component, composed of you and your staff, with *your* particular jurisdiction and accountability in the life of the agency

However, it's not always as neat as that. As you'll see when we get into the text, the jurisdictions frequently intersect and the differences become blurred. Thus, the question of authority arises as to which component should respond to and decide on the various affairs and concerns of the agency. It's not always clear, and this tends to cause tension between the two components. So that drives me to make one more point here at the beginning: Don't be too easily intimidated by your subordinate status.

Throughout the text, you'll encounter my suggestions that with respect to certain matters, you should "demand" or "insist" or "see to it that." This implies that you have such a right—*and you do!* You may be subordinate to the board of trustees, *but you are the agency's principal entrepreneur.* (Is "entrepreneuse" the feminine form of that word?) Although the board exercises the ultimate authority with respect to the agency, you exercise the immediate authority. *So go girl (or guy). Use it!*

The second motivation is pure sentiment. It is to record my gratitude to a few of the human beings who personified the spirit of that which every nonprofit organization—large or small, no matter how complex its trappings—should strive to achieve. That is, holding out its hand to someone in some kind of need, and offering help with no thought of personal gain. One of them was my Uncle Louie. If I did not mention him in these pages, his name would be forever forgotten. I strongly believe that the whole nonprofit world should just be a way of institutionalizing good neighborliness such as he showed to my family and me. This nonprofit world of ours could well have started with one family of cave dwellers borrowing a cup of sugar from a nearby family of cave dwellers. (Incidentally, over the years, I've seen hundreds of incidents of borrowed sugar, but never was one paid back.)

The story of Uncle Louie goes back several decades—actually, to late August of 1936. The country was trying to dig itself out of the Great Depression. Our families—Uncle Louie's and mine—lived across the street from each other. We had no money, and it was hardly likely that I'd realize my ambition of going to college. Moreover, Hamilton College had just informed me that even though I was selected for admission to the freshman class, my application for scholarship aid had been rejected. At the tender age of 16, I was crushed.

Uncle Louie, who had no formal education, was earning his living the hard way, as a school building custodian. He called me over to his house where he lived with my Aunt Celia, my father's sister, and handed me $20 in cash—real cash. He said, "You're the first one in the family to go to college. Go to it. Show us the way. Here's some pocket money; I'm betting on you." That's what made me overcome my pessimism. Twenty dollars was a lot of money then. I went up to the college campus in Clinton, New York, two days later, enrolled for five courses and three part-time jobs, and hung on for that first difficult and frightening semester simply because Uncle Louie was "betting on" me. I went to see the dean, the college's sole dean. (There's a frightening number of deans and chancellors and provosts in almost every college these days.) I told him that I had a financial problem that I hoped to be able to overcome by my part-time jobs. I also made the point that the jobs might detract from my classroom accomplishments, but that I'd try my best. Then, emboldened by I don't know what—probably Uncle Louis's $20 bet—I suggested to him that if my grades after one semester were better than those of any freshman to whom the college had awarded an academic scholarship, I'd expect my scholarship application to be reconsidered. Can you imagine? He agreed.

After that semester, the scholarship aid started rolling in. But for each of the seven semesters thereafter, Uncle Louie never forgot to call me over and hand me another $20 for "pocket money." When I graduated from college, I went quickly into the military (five years of that). By the time I was mustered out, Uncle Louie was gone, so I never had the chance to tell him of the strength of his influence on me, and my gratitude for his generosity for which he never expected a return. Now I'm telling you. That's what it's all about, isn't it?

Although the text of this book is divided into lessons, not every lesson will teach you something. In some, I have departed from instruction to narration—the mere telling of a story. Life in the nonprofit world, in fact in *any* world, has its funny nooks and crannies, and I'm disclosing some of those to you. So some lessons are presented just for fun. And every once in a while, I'll introduce you to other characters who played some wonderful part in my history by representing the humane qualities that remind me of the basics of what the nonprofit universe should mean to us all.

As to my own human qualities, I want you to know something about my early life because it was so unusual. That, in turn, forged in me some unusual approaches that frequently emerge in my writing and my thinking. If I do not mouth the usual homilies about the nonprofit world, remember—you've been forewarned. I once considered writing my autobiography, and I planned to entitle it, *If You Don't Behave Yourself, You Can't Go to Gus Van's Funeral*. I suppose that requires a bit of explanation, and here it is.

My father, as is the case with all fathers, said lots of things to me by way of advice or discipline. But the title to this non-lesson is one of his enjoinders that I shall not forget. Obviously, I have not forgotten it in 70 years, because it happened when I was 11. The year was 1930, and my brother Stanley and I were vaudevillians. We were the "kid act" known as "The Happiness Kids," and we enjoyed what was then considered artistic success, traveling across the eastern half of the United States with troupes that included the Marx Brothers, Fanny Brice, and Ben Blue. Our act originated in 1924, when I was five, and our song and dance career lasted until 1931. The end came that summer when we were about to do a booking, a gig, at a big New York vaudeville house. But before we could start our performance, our parents were arrested on the charge of contributing to our truancy. My father called the charge a trivial technicality—he had inadvertently forgotten to enroll us in school. Stanley and I were both, incidentally, completely literate, had significant checking accounts, had been supporting our parents for seven years, and knew intimately the geography and the train schedules of the entire eastern half of the country.

My father's explanation was so naively disarming that our parents were put on probation on condition that we be enrolled in school by the beginning of the next school year in September of 1931. That was prior to the counseling rage that we find in schools today, so I was summarily assigned to the first grade. I was bemused by the day's events, particularly by the number of six-year-olds who were wetting their pants. And I noted that I was then the tallest kid in the group, something I savored because it was the last time in my life that I could claim that fame. When after a few weeks they moved me to the sixth grade, I lost that distinction, and at my full adult height of 5'4," I've never regained it.

To call the vaudeville part of my life unorthodox is an understatement. It was an unreality: three-a-day shows sometimes, running for trains, sleeping in flea bag hotels on occasion, and trying to eat and avoid ptomaine poisoning at the same time. But as kids, we didn't notice all of that. I think we had fun, and many in our troupe became our friends and, irrespective of age differences, treated us like equals. But sometimes, as kids will, we acted up. And that leads to the title of this non-lesson.

At that time, when a vaudevillian died, the colleagues in the "profession" took it upon themselves to do two things: chip in to pay for the funeral (vaudevillians all lived above their means) and come together at the funeral parlor for a rollicking performance of their routines to send the decedent off with "a big finish." Sometime in 1930, Gus Van, known as

"Van, the Melody Man" and part of the team of Van and Schenk, died. The world of vaudeville geared up for the occasion of what would be a marathon performance by the best of the entertainers of the era—Eddie Cantor, Al Jolson, Fred and Gracie Allen—you name them and they were there. Somehow, I must have been misbehaving in a way that called for discipline. It must have been serious. My father lectured me on my derelictions, then for a long moment, pondered my punishment. Finally, he issued his decree: If you don't behave yourself, you can't go to Gus Van's funeral.

This may be the most bizarre form of punishment ever meted out to an 11-year-old. Perhaps it can give you some insight into the warped sense of humor that, my wife Joanne reminds me, can here and there be detected in this book.

PREFACE TO THE LESSONS: LET'S TURN TO MYTHOLOGY

I have two different academic appointments at two different institutions of higher education. At one, I have a professorship in trusteeship; I teach a graduate school course on the subject to master's degree candidates who aspire to be EDs of some agency or other when they graduate. At the other, I teach the only inner-city community college course in the country in Greek tragedy and mythology. Coincidentally, there's a lot of mythology in the concept of trusteeship, and one way of presenting some of the lessons is to cite the myth and then explode it. That's what I'll be doing from time to time in this text. To a certain extent, I regret having to do so, because most myths are poetic and romantic and quite moving and beautiful. But myths, not realities, about leadership in the nonprofit world can be misleading and harmful.

CHAPTER 1

Getting Started on the Right Foot

H ere are a few thoughts to get you past some potential toe-stubbers that frequently trip up the unwary. In essence, these initial lessons emphasize your role as *boss*, a role that all too often is approached with too much uncertainty. Gather up your energies, principles, ingenuity, and plain horse sense and start up (not down) the path. Don't be distracted too soon by pulls and pushes of conflicting expectations, rumors, or infusions of comments masquerading as advice. Keep your own counsel. You're in charge. And remember the enjoinder in that old Russian proverb: Since when does the fiddle pick the tune?

LESSON 1—DON'T LET THE BOARD MESS AROUND WITH MISSION

An Important First Step

As a general rule, boards of trustees, unless otherwise influenced by you and the board chair, seem to feel more comfortable dealing with little issues than with big ones—little issues are more easily disposed of and give the board a more immediate feeling of achievement. Quite naturally, it's easier to make a decision about mending the roof leaks than it is to determine how to confront societal changes. So boards virtually leap at the chance to reexamine the mere verbiage of the mission statement, if that opportunity ever presents itself. And they can get lost in the task. Boards have a tendency to be more at ease going back over familiar territory, familiar issues, than going forward to new challenges. There's one rule for this situation: *Don't let them do it.*

Your mission statement should have two elements and only two elements: (a) what you're going to do and (b) for whom. That's all. Save the poetry for another document—like the annual report or that big funding proposal. Avoid the tyranny of adjectives. Every time you add an adjective or descriptive phrase to your mission statement, you open the possibility for an argument that could go either way: (a) It *restricts* your intended functioning or, inexplicably, (b) it *expands* your intended functioning. That very same adjective can be the basis for either position. Very frequently, a nonprofit agency, through its board, is compelled to justify the agency's actions regarding goals or programs. Someone may question the board's duty of loyalty to the agency's mission. The point to be made here is that you and your board want, simply *must have*, the freedom of interpretation—one of your most important functions in meeting changing community needs and yet balancing them against your already established mission statement. Adjectives only complicate the problem, so stop embellishing. Embellishing intrudes on that freedom.

Further, *don't* include in your mission statement the steps that you'll take to achieve your goal. That belongs in the "programs" sections of your institutional plan or long-range plan or three-year plan, or whatever you call it. I'll cover the "plan" stuff later, in Lesson 11. If the mission statement that you have now states with reasonable accuracy what you're doing and for whom, *hands off.*

Somewhere on the next page or two, you'll find my idea of a not-so-good mission statement and a good mission statement. So take it from there. Never mind, I've decided that we'll take it on right here. Let's use this handy example.

Here is the original mission statement for a nonprofit agency with which I recently consulted: "Our mission is to help all of those suffering alcoholics and addicts who have a genuine willingness to change their lives." Taken in its entirety, it exudes good intentions—no argument about that. But it invites too much debate, and here's how I'd change it. I'm going to italicize the words that I'd eliminate: "Our mission is to help *all of those suffering* alcoholics and addicts *who have a genuine willingness to change their lives.*" Thus, after the eliminations, we end up with a simple eight-word declaratory sentence that states what we're going to do and for whom. Let's get silly for a moment. Here's what we've avoided.

An ultra-fussy trustee, donor, foundation, or other stakeholder of small mind and literal bent on

1. claiming that if you don't help all in that category, you're violating your mission and don't deserve continued support;

2. claiming that if the alcoholics and addicts whom you are helping are not *suffering* (perhaps at this point they're enjoying themselves), or if they haven't been clearly identified as persons *who have a willingness to change their lives*, then here too you're violating your mission and don't deserve continued support;

or

3. claiming that if the alcoholics and addicts whom you are helping are indeed *suffering* and even *have a willingness to change their lives* but you can't prove that *willingness* to be *genuine*, then here too you're vi-

olating your mission and don't deserve continued support.

Agreed? Well, you get the point. So let's not continue this idiocy any longer. Just remember—KISS—keep it simple, sister: what you're going to do and for whom. That's your mission statement.

Thus, in my example, we've moved from "Our mission is to help all of those suffering alcoholics and addicts who have a genuine willingness to change their lives" to "Our mission is to help alcoholics and addicts."

LESSON 2—IF YOU'RE THE FIRST EXECUTIVE DIRECTOR OF AN ALREADY FUNCTIONING AGENCY

Combating Founder's Disease

This could cause ulcers for all concerned. The likelihood is that if you're the first executive director (ED) of an established and functioning agency, you're facing the issue of how to handle what I'll call a "founding board." A founding board is identified by its functioning, not necessarily by *when* it functions in the agency's chronological life. Somebody gets a good idea about meeting a particular need in the community—perhaps a temporary shelter for runaway teenagers. To get it started, he puts up some of his own money. Then he gets some more money from friends and well-wishers, and then a bit more from a sympathetic foundation. He enlists close friends to serve on his board and they all participate with new, fresh enthusiasm in the functioning of the agency. The trustees take it upon themselves to do everything that has to be done in the agency's operations—from declaring its policies to inventorying its paper clips. Thus, they are a "founding board" in the context that it's a new organization and they're the first trustees. But note this: The term "founding board" is not necessarily related to *newness* at all. It really applies to a board that takes it upon itself to do everything that has to be done in the agency's operations—dealing only rarely with policy, but much more frequently with paper clips. So, functionally it is a founding board, because it hasn't matured into the next, more desirable phase of being a "governing board." It may not even be a new organization. I have dealt with agencies that are several decades old, but their boards are still founding boards, functionally speaking. And here's where you come in.

The trustees now decide that there's just too much to do and they need a professional staff. And for the moment, you're it. Most times, although they may have thought out what they'd like you to do, they haven't thought out what that will mean in terms of requiring them to *change* their role to that of a real-life "governing board"—one that governs, not one that now continues to administer or manage. I italicized the word "change" in the previous sentence for the specific purpose of pursuing a point. Change is a troublesome challenge to most people: It comes hard to every human enterprise. You'd think that we'd be over that syndrome by now simply because change is inevitable, we experience it every day and in every relationship, and we freely acknowledge both of these ideas. Frequently, we old birds express a preference for the "good old days." (They may have been good, but were they really better?) But we go along with the change anyway. Right? No, not at all. We can answer "yes" when it comes to almost any other aspect of our lives, but not when it comes to a fundamental change in our beloved nonprofit organization.

Modify our mission? Hell, no! The community loves us just as we are. Expand or diversify the board? Never! Look at how well we get along. We agree on everything. Why bring in a bunch of outsiders? (And then there's the "really big one," as Ed Sullivan used to say in introducing his star performer of the evening.) Here, in our case, the "really big one" is whether or not we should employ a professional leader, an ED. Hell, no! (Again!) We trustees have been running this place for 102 years. Why the sudden change?

Well, readers, the change is not as sudden as one may think. Surely, for 102 years, the board *has* been running the place, but not entirely on its own. There's been a bookkeeper and a switchboard operator and a general secretary/filing clerk/stenographer, but that's all as far as "professional staff" is concerned. But, those three could never be considered professional *leadership.* So now we're at today and all that today implies for the nonprofit agency that wants to remain alive and vital, vibrant and relevant. We're starting to experience programmatic complications, increased burdens of fundraising, donor demands for both effective planning and procedures for evaluating every aspect of agency functioning, and just the innumerable administrative steps of keeping the board alive, in communication, active, and productive.

So it goes. But then someone makes the suggestion at the next board meeting that it might be "advisable" to have one of those newfangled professional folks (that's going to be you) sharing the leadership mantle. In much less articulate language than I am now using to describe what he actually says, he argues that we're getting to the point where someone may actually have to devote paid-for time to the endless issues of management. These are the issues that have taken so much of our attention and energies away from the still bigger issues. That suggestion will probably evoke the liveliest discussion that the board will ever have had. First, the board will have to deal with the symptoms of what we in the nonprofit world call "founder's disease." This refers to the old veterans of the agency trying to hold to a certain, previously held course no matter what the consequence internally (how it affects administrative and programmatic functions) or externally (what it means in possibly obsolete service to the community). The disease is based on two factors: well-meaning and well-deserved pride in what they have accomplished all these years, and the very fear of change, especially the type of change that cuts into authority. But in our scenario, let's assume that the veterans lose out on this one. So now we have a chance to peek in on what happens next in the context of (a) their decision, at last, to employ a first ED, and (b) the bumps and bruises of their not doing the necessary planning for the traumatic transition. This is the transition to which I referred before—from that of a founding board to that of a governing board. It can really be hell.

In the recent past, I was engaged to work with two different nonprofit agencies, each of which had just hired its first ED—one of them after 85 years without professional leadership, and the other after 103 years without it. The first was a model of how things should be done (my rules as to this follow later in this lesson). The second was less than a success, and for the new ED, the experience was, in her own words, "a personal purgatory." Let's look into that second agency, and we can note the giveaway signs that from the very beginning of the process of bringing on board a first ED should have told them that things would be tough.

1.   During those 103 years, the board chair role was played by a person who held the additional title of "president." That term, in my mind, implies a *managerial* position, one of day-to-day authority and attention to day-to-day details. This was of course consistent with the board's functioning as a founding board, but it was also a foreboding of problems still to come. When I came on the scene, the president had her presidential office in the agency's building and the agency's secretary/filing clerk/stenographer was considered the president's own secretary/filing clerk/stenographer. That president, when asked her profession, declared "the presidency of ABC agency." At this point, when

the new ED appeared for duty, she was assigned a smaller office next to that of the president, and was told that she'd have to share the services of "the president's secretary."

2.   The tentative job description for the new ED referred to her authority as to junior staff in rather equivocal fashion. She was to "clear" all decisions relating to staff with the board's employment committee. Regarding this issue, her first decision concerning the employment of one junior staff person and her second decision concerning the discharge of another were overruled by that board committee. Are you getting the picture?

3.   The minor ministerial decisions that she made and, out of a sense of insecurity, reported to the board at its meetings, were the subject of painfully long discussions as to her "real authority."

4.   Junior staff answered her questions in grumbling fashion and did her bidding only with open resentment.

What's wrong with this picture? Practically everything. But basically, if the board was indeed willing to move its own status from that of a founding board to that of a governing board, it is then incumbent on *you—before you accept that ED position*—to assure yourself that it could adopt for itself, and inculcate in the others in the agency, the mindset that allows that to happen successfully.

Well, here are some caveats for you to follow, and not all of them are easy.

1.   Have a serious heart-to-heart with the leaders of the group to make sure the trustees are ready to move from being a *founding* board to being a *governing* board.

2. Make sure the trustees are ready to give up the heady pleasure of day-to-day control—that they're ready to disengage from management-level decisions. Tell them, as you and I have already agreed, that they still have the ultimate authority, but that you must have the immediate authority; that they have the accountability, but that you'll undertake most of the responsibilities that underlay their accountability.

3. Insist on a written job description for yourself that clearly reflects what I've stated in numbers 1 and 2 above. In any case, there is no alternative to giving the new ED complete authority over the employment and discharge of staff serving under her. This is *not* a board function at this point in its life.

4. Insist that the president relinquish her self-perceived and board-perceived status as chief executive of the agency. Although I dislike getting into this type of detail, that means giving up her office space and secretarial support and giving up the mindset that her position with the agency is her "profession." It no longer is, but it's another, and equally gratifying status in her life—the honor of being board chair of an agency that (we hope) represents her third romance. More on that "romance" thing later.

5. Make it clear to the board that you do not expect to bring to the board table for discussion the subject of your ministerial decisions, except as they may eventually pertain to the board's deliberations on the agency's mission-related or goal-related matters. Management-related issues are, in general, yours to decide.

6. Make it clear that it is the board's responsibility to create an agency-wide mindset in which the

change can take place with the least possible tension and confrontation. Not only must the board itself support the change, but the board must manifest that support by carefully and persuasively communicating that fact to other constituencies—staff and volunteers, most importantly—and further communicating what is now expected of them in the new environment that they're creating by bringing you on.

7.   Expect and tolerate some leftover meddling on the part of a few of the old timers until you can get through Lesson 4 of this book. Usually, they're well-meaning folks, and they did, after all, have the foresight and the altruism to get the place going and build the partitions and paint the walls and sweep the floors and make the sandwiches for the kids who went there.

8.   With respect to their ultimate authority, give the trustees a few generalities to go on until they get to feel comfortable (a) about your presence, (b) about sharing with you the agency's leadership, and (c) about trying to establish some semblance of a protocol regarding board turf versus ED/staff turf. Here are a few such generalities. No one of them will resolve the issue, but you'll get the point and so will they. The first is called the Queen Victoria approach: "The board *reigns* but it does not *rule*." (This is said dramatically, with arms outstretched to their full length.) The second is called the blue-collar approach: "No one on the board should perform any duties that someone on staff is paid to do." The third is the well-known anatomical approach: "With respect to the affairs of the agency, the trustees should keep their noses in but their fingers out." Don't be surprised if you have to repeat these adages from time to time. I'm

putting them in quotation marks because I've heard them stated frequently, but I haven't the slightest idea who originated them. I do know, however, that they did not originate with me. So, while I can't make a positive attribution, I'm not claiming personal credit for them.

I'm pleased to tell you that the first agency followed all of these procedures. The change for it was by no means seamless, but it worked. As to the second agency, I worked diligently in an after-the-fact manner to overcome the mistakes that were made before I was engaged to help.

The ED survived her purgatory. But did she get a glimpse of heaven after I finished? No, I'm not *that* good a consultant.

Obviously, these are merely guidelines. Don't become too enamored of them. See Lesson 15 for their limitations.

LESSON 3—TRUSTEES ARE NOT VOLUNTEERS, SO DON'T TREAT THEM AS SUCH

Hold their Feet to the Fire, or, the First Myth

"Listen, I'm just a volunteer."

I've heard it a thousand times from trustees who want either sympathy for their donations of time or perhaps an excuse for (say) missing meetings or not helping in soliciting financial support for the organization. When a trustee makes such a claim, he or she is relying on one of the myths that underlay trusteeship—one of the five myths that I'm obligated to explode. It's rubbish!

There is a legal definition—or better still, a description—for a trustee's role, and it goes something like this: a person to whom resources are assigned for the purpose of being used for the benefit of another. In the case of the nonprofit agency, the "person" in question is the board of trustees, and the "purpose" is that of being used for the benefit of society or some segment of society as specified in the mission statement. And the word "assigned" implies that the assignee (board of trustees) has (a) ownership of the resources, hence (b) a legal interest in them, and, hence (c) authority over them. Further, the ownership factor carries with it areas of accountability, both individually as to each trustee and collectively as to the board as a whole. Those areas of accountability, in the aggregate, make up an implied job description for trustees that is more onerous than your own.

By comparison, the definition of a volunteer (originating in the Latin, *voluntare*, to do only what one elects to do) is somewhat like this: one who undertakes to perform a task—period! The clear implication is that with respect to the "volunteer," there is no necessary ownership of or other legal interest in, or necessary authority over, the matter. If boards of trustees were allowed to consider themselves in that category, and many trustees do, the nonprofit world would be in a "helluva" shape. My enjoinder to you is as follows, but my editor won't allow me to present it in solid capitals: *Don't ever refer to any of your trustees as a "volunteer."* But even more important, don't ever *defer* to any of your trustees as if he/she were a volunteer.

There should be a job description for trustees just as there should be for any person or group occupying a position of trust or responsibility. In the literature of the nonprofit world, there are scores of versions of such descriptions, but I'm including here a summary of the one that I've found to be the best of the lot. I submit this to you with reference to Lesson 6, wherein I ascribe to you the responsibility of being the principal educator of your board of trustees. You must see to it that what follows here is clearly and emphatically communicated to them.

It's set forth in more detail in a 26-page pamphlet written by Dr. Richard T. (Tom) Ingram, president of the Association of Governing Boards of Universities and Colleges (AGB), and published in 1996 by the National Center for Nonprofit Boards. I met Tom when he was a vice president of AGB; I served on AGB's board for nine years, one as its chairman. The title of his work is *Ten Basic Responsibilities of Nonprofit Boards,* but it's really a lot more than the title implies. First, he lists the 13 areas of responsibility of a board of trustees *while acting as a board—collectively, that is.* Then, he lists the 22 responsibilities devolving on *the individual trustee* just by virtue of *being a trustee.* Considering the mere magnitude of those numbers, it should be pretty clear to all of us that a trustee who undertakes that burden cannot be considered a volunteer. Obviously, a person has the privilege of accepting or rejecting board service, but once a person has accepted, he/she has exhausted his/her options—non-performance is not an option. Let's keep our own feet to the fire by noting here and now what Tom specifies (Exhibit 1–1).

There it is, so go to it. But for heaven's sake, don't just hand it to your currently serving trustees cold turkey and say that this is what you expect of them. The likely reaction to such a move is resignation, a fainting spell, or a few well-seasoned remarks about your hubris. Instead, use your board chair as your interference just as the running back uses the fullback to do his blocking. (Forgive me. From here on, I'm going to continue to refer to the board chair in the masculine and the ED in the feminine; that's the usual *dramatis personnae.* If you want to call me on that, please feel free to do so. You have my e-mail address.) Here we need a mindset that is probably vastly different from the mindset that I had (I'm using me only as an example here) when I was first induced to become a board member.

Exhibit 1–1 Areas of Responsibility

For the Board as a Board

1. Determine the organization's mission and purpose.

2. Select the chief executive.

3. Support the chief executive.

4. Assess the chief executive's performance.

5. Ensure effective organizational planning.

6. Ensure adequate resources.

7. Manage resources effectively.

8. Determine, monitor, and strengthen the organization's programs and services.

9. Enhance the organization's public standing.

10. Ensure legal and ethical integrity.

11. Maintain accountability.

12. Recruit and orient new board members.

13. Assess board performance.

For the Individual Trustee

1. General expectations

   • Know all aspects of the organization.

   • Display competence in performing duties of care, loyalty, and obedience.

   • Suggest nominees for board membership.

   • Serve in leadership positions and undertake special assignments.

   • Avoid prejudiced judgments based on outside information.

   • Bring goodwill to the board's deliberations.

(continues)

Exhibit 1–1 Continued

2. Meetings

   - Prepare for and participate in them.
   - Ask substantive questions.
   - Support majority decisions.
   - Maintain confidentiality of board's executive sessions.
   - Speak for the organization only when authorized to do so.
   - Suggest agenda items for board and committee meetings.

3. Relationship with staff

   - Counsel with the executive director and support him/her in difficulties with groups or individuals.
   - Avoid asking special favors of staff.
   - Avoid asking for extensive, voluminous information.

4. Avoiding conflicts

   - Do not "represent a constituency" at the board table.
   - Immediately disclose any possible conflict of interest or what might appear to be a conflict of interest.
   - Never accept favors from, or offer favors to, anyone doing business with the organization.

5. Fiduciary responsibilities

   - Emphasize to the board prudence with respect to its funds.
   - Faithfully read and understand the organizational financial statements.

6. Fundraising

   - Give an annual gift in accordance with personal means.
   - Personally assist in all fundraising strategies.

At that time, I was probably approached in the softest manner: "Come on Lewis, we'd like to have you on our board for our home for runaway girls. We're all friends. It's good for your resume. We have six board meetings a year and you don't have to come to all of them. You'll serve on a committee and you'll give $200 each year to the annual fund. If we have a capital campaign, you'll go out, pump some hands, and chase down $10,000 from your friends and business associates. Besides, you'll have a chance at some deft networking (wink, wink). That's all there is to it."

Well obviously, as you look at that onerous job description, you realize that that *isn't* all there is to it. This is serious stuff. In fact, I'd prefer putting it to the trustee candidate in a completely different way. I'd like to see him/her approached with the thought that serving on your board ought to be the third full-time commitment and romance in his/her life. The first is the candidate's family and peripheral family activities—the home life and the skating lessons and the violin lessons and the Girl Scouts/Boy Scouts and the religious affiliation. The second is the candidate's mode of earning a living. And the third is your agency and its mission. And if you want to be honest and candid with your candidate, that's what you ought to say. And if the candidate concludes that the agency and its mission occupies a place lower than his/her third romance, perhaps you should withdraw the invitation (see Appendix A).

Earlier in this lesson, I referred to the technique of you using your board chair as interference when presenting to the trustees their job description after the fact of their having joined on. There's nothing evil in that "interference" expression.

Well, that thought brings us to the next lesson.

LESSON 4—EXPLOIT YOUR BOARD CHAIR

This is a *Real* Wow!

Don't worry about my use of the word "exploit"—there's nothing insidious about it. In its best use, it means "to turn a resource to good account," and that's exactly what we're considering here. Your board chair is your richest resource. (Of course, this works only if he knows *his* real chunk of the leadership role. That's another issue, but this book is for you, not him.)

After your spousal or spousal-equivalent relationship, the right relationship between you and your board chair is probably the next most important one because it can make or break your success as an ED. It could also mean the difference between an agency that fulfills its mission and one that doesn't. No, I'm not suggesting that you be obsequious, obedient, or sycophantic. In fact, you may have to be tough and quick to express your disagreement. But the object of this exercise is to create between the two of you an arrangement that I call "a benign conspiracy." By benign, I mean gracious, or of gentle disposition. By conspiracy, I do *not* mean anything devious or arcane. You're not going to plot against, or keep secrets from, the rest of the board. I mean instead to emphasize the two distinct Latin-based syllabic origins of that word ("con" and "spira") and come out with the very positive meaning of conspiracy, that is *"aspiring* together," hoping together, dreaming together. That sounds rather noble, doesn't it? And by this I am referring to the two topmost figures in the agency—you and the board chair—sharing your aspirations and working together to see that the board *and* the staff *and* everyone else involved in the delivery of the agency's services is going along with the dynamics that you and he launch. You're going to see to it (there's the phrase that you're going to see and hear frequently) that the board of trustees is operating at the proper level of governance and preoccupying itself with the agency's mission-related and goal-related issues—the big issues that will create impacts on, and even challenge, its very existence, not the roof leaks and parking lot repairs.

I don't have any undiscovered secrets for how you're going to create this environment between you and the board chair. But going back to the subject at hand, whatever your talents are for fostering mutual trust, mutual confidence, mutual respect, and even mutual affection, they will certainly help here. And once established, this benign conspiracy now becomes the key to some of the other lessons in this book.

So, as an example, if you feel that your trustees need some form of a job description to help them understand their real role in the life of the agency, in your benign conspiracy sessions with your board chair, you will soon conclude that the idea would probably be more acceptable if it "originated" with him. And he would then announce to the other trustees that he has requested that you, the ED, do some research on the matter and bring to the board at some future meeting a draft of what *you* believe to represent the best practices on the issue. Get it?

And that benign conspiracy comes in handy in other situations, as well. When one of the old leftovers from the board's "founding" phase starts to nettle you by getting into micromanagement (see Lesson 2), you'll report that to your board chair during one of your benign conspiracy sessions and *he, not you,* will take it from there. That's sharing leadership the right way. And you'll see that he, your chair, is going to be your key player when we soon get to Lesson 6. You'll meet it again in Lesson 14 on creating and enacting policy, and also Lesson 16a on the comedy of errors that we sometimes refer to as board meetings, and, most importantly, Lesson 17, which requires that we differentiate ourselves from the for-profit world.

LESSON 5—DON'T BLAME THE TRUSTEES FOR BEING NAIVE ABOUT TRUSTEESHIP

You've Got a Job Here

This all starts with a profound irony, so be sympathetic, at least for a while and until you and your board chair really get that benign conspiracy thing working. Here's the big irony of the nonprofit world. The board of trustees, with the agency's highest level of accountability, has the least training for its role. I'll illustrate the point with a scenario. I like scenarios and I write plays just so I can create them.

Digression: My plays all feature women: Pocahontas, Rosa Parks, and Elena. Elena was a virtually unknown Spartan slave whom I cast as the only woman ever to perform in plays in ancient Athens. In *my* play, I give her a leading role in one of the plays of Aeschylus. But for now, let's take as our scenario the traditional nonprofit hospital (we're assuming that there still is one of that species left). No question about it: All of the people in every cohort of the agency who are involved in the delivery of its services—physician, nursing, pharmaceutical, administrative, maintenance (you name it)—are carefully and professionally trained for the respective tasks devolving on them. But the board of trustees—the one component of the agency that is entirely responsible, answerable, and accountable (I'm going to have to refer to this word in a separate lesson) to the community for ensuring that each such person in each such cohort performs adequately (nay, commendably)—yes, the board of trustees is the only component of the agency that is not professionally trained for the task devolving on *it*. When I get real angry about this reality, I contend to my graduate students that many trustees are recruited for board membership by a method that crosses deceit with seduction. I've already explained this in Lesson 3.

You'll see more fully what I mean when you compare this palaver with the trustees' job description that I mentioned in Lessons 3 and 4. Okay, okay—you don't have to tell me. If you want me on your board and you hand me that job description and ask if I'm willing to sign on, the likelihood is that I'll laugh in your face. So maybe that's the extreme way of trying to recruit me. But that's extreme honesty. The other way is complete deception and let's me get away with thinking that I'm just a volunteer.

LESSON 6—YOU ARE THE PRIME EDUCATOR TO YOUR BOARD

They are Looking to You

I have to make something clear here. I've alluded to it and implied it, but not said it with sufficient emphasis. Yet it undergirds much of what I'm telling you. The "it" is this: *YOU ARE THE PRINCIPAL EDUCATOR OF YOUR BOARD.* (I got away with the solid caps this time. I guess my editor wasn't looking.) So when, for example, I tell you that the trustees' feet must be held to the fire, or that they are not volunteers, or that their turf consists of the mission-related and goal-related concerns of the agency, or that there's an onerous job description that they must fulfill, *you're* the one who must, in turn, tell *them* the very same things. Okay? So let's go on from here.

About continuing the irony of how trustees are "recruited," you must now get your benign conspiracy mechanism working and work out with your board chair how to ensure that the recruits have a realistic view of what is expected of them. This is one of the aspects of the concept of "ownership" that plays such an important role in the life of nonprofit leadership. But I'll go into that concept in the next lesson. I want this one to be short and to the point. So please memorize the third sentence of the previous paragraph in this lesson (the part of the sentence in solid capitals) and I'll be satisfied. Now we'll pick up this theme in Lesson 7.

CHAPTER 2

Remembering Roles

This is a tricky one. Throughout this book, I dwell on leadership roles—the sometimes separate, sometimes combined roles of board and staff as influenced by the ever-changing niceties that define exactly *who* is supposed to do exactly *what* on a particular occasion or in response to a particular issue. Herein I discuss some of the details. But there's one of which you must be ever mindful: With respect to whatever role devolves on your board, you may have to play the extra role of informing them just what it is. That sometimes makes a mockery of the theory that you're subordinate to your board, doesn't it?

LESSON 7—THE BOARD OWNS THE AGENCY

What That Means

This is a long lesson, longer than I wanted it to be, so maybe you should read it in more than one sitting.

Frequently, when I do consultancies out in the field, I ask my trustee audience, "Who owns this enterprise?" Just as frequently, my question evokes some mumbling, then hesitatingly, someone and then someone else ventures answers that really have the intonation of questions: The state? The public? The students? The patients? Here again, I enjoin you: You will have to instruct your board (through the chair, of course) on everything I'm telling you here. First, make sure they understand that *they own* the agency. Obviously, they hold that ownership position as a public trust (they may not realize that, either), but they own it nonetheless. The two most important, and interrelated as you will see, muniments of ownership are (a) that the board has the *privilege* of determining the agency's role in helping to improve society, but conversely, (b) that the board has the *obligation* of determining the agency's role in helping to improve society.

Now let me show off a little: I retrieved the word "muniments" from my 1836 edition of *Blackstone's Commentaries on the Laws of England,* a 12-pound tome that I used to carry around on New York subways in 1941, just before I abandoned the study of law to enlist in military service, the day after Pearl Harbor. I'll tell you more about that later—but back to you.

The concept of ownership applies—and this is at the *wow!* level of importance—also to the board's ownership of *its own functioning.* It must take strong hold of all of the dynamics that affect its effectiveness as a governing body. I suggest that this be done by disbanding the board's nominating committee (it seems that every board has one) and creating in its place the board's most important committee—I'll call it the committee on governance or on trusteeship or on board development or whatever. It will be empowered to tend to the five most important aspects of trusteeship with which the board must deal. Dealing with each aspect requires a special "mechanism," and now I'm going to list them and comment on each. Getting the board (through the chair) to agree to this won't be as hard a sell as you suspect. Try it, you'll see. Just assure the chair that you'll give that committee all of the staff support it needs. And it will need a lot.

Mechanism I: The Recruitment Mechanism

Make it clear to your board that you as ED can get the governance-level support that you deserve (and must have to do *your* job effectively) only when the trustees understand what is expected of them in their board service. Clearly, on-the-job training isn't enough, and you don't have to settle for it. There has to be some understanding in advance so you don't suffer a lot of disappointed expectancies. You deserve better.

So what about having the members of the new committee hand the prospective member a copy of our now-infamous job description for a trustee? And what about their saying, "Here's what we expect of you. If you agree to these terms, come on our board. If you don't, don't!"

Well, guys, as I've said before, not even *I* recommend that crude an approach. (But let me interject this: If you tried that with 50 candidates and 45 turned you down, you'd probably have one dynamite board with just those other five.) But there's a middle ground. At the very least, make sure the candidate

1. is familiar with:

   - your mission statement

   - the goals and objectives in your institutional/ long-range plan, or whatever you call it

   - the aspirations of your development plan, or whatever you call *it*

   - the provisions of your code of regulations (some of you call them bylaws)

   - all of your policy declarations

2.   has expressed his/her intentions to comport with all of it, including his/her commitment as to:

- meeting attendance

- meeting participation

- committee service

- financial support

- faithfully reading all of the material that you send out on behalf of the agency, as preparation for meetings

I haven't talked about the widespread and fashionable issue of a board "profile." You know what I mean—trying to match trustee types with the agency's future needs at the board level. There are all kinds of fancy grids set forth in the literature to help you in that feckless exercise. They suggest to you that if you're going through a building expansion phase, you may need one construction engineer, one banker, one mortgage broker, one lawyer, one accountant and, just to add spice and the requisite diversity, one woman, one Hispanic American, one African American, one Jewish American, and one...well, why go on with this? Except for the idea of diversity, with which I agree wholeheartedly, I disagree with the idea of having "specialty trustees." I don't want trustees second guessing your decisions on programmatic issues, and neither do you. If you need a construction engineer (or a banker, a mortgage broker, a lawyer, an accountant, or whatever) to help you carry out a board-approved construction project, have your board furnish the resources so you can engage whom and what you need. Then there isn't even the hint to justify any perceived or suspected conflict of interest. And besides, we're trying to keep the trustees away from day-to-day matters, aren't we? We (you and I) want them to operate as trustees, not as administrators.

Digression: Funny thing about construction projects—the trustees just *love* to get into the detail of color schemes and window treatments and roof tiles, and then, later, into carpeting and furniture. It's as if they have this one last time to trot out their memories of early life with their erector sets. The only "specialty" that you should demand of those selected by your governance committee is that of a special passion for your mission.

Mechanism II: The Orientation Mechanism

Much of what I covered in Mechanism I also applies here. I've consulted with boards, some members of which have responded "no" to my question, "Are you familiar with the agency's mission statement?" Imagine! In my mind, I then ask, "Why in hell (those last two words are discretionary, not required) are you on this board if there's nothing to which you can attach your passion? Or don't you have any passion for the mission in the first place?"

At the very least, you must insist that your board have an orientation process that familiarizes the new trustee with all of the organizational and governance documents cited above, as well as some recent board minutes, minutes of significant committees, financial statements, and annual reports. And let's throw in a visit to the facilities and a couple of reminiscence-loaded luncheons with you and a few of the old timers. Tell your governance committee members to use those opportunities to talk about vision and dreams for the future as well as—and not just—the culture of the past.

Mechanism III: The Engagement Mechanism

This one interrelates with the first two. It's the set of activities devised by your governance committee to see to it that every new trustee hits the ground running. When Ms. Adams sits in stony and uncomfortable silence at her first three quarter-annual board meetings, I ask her "why?" She tells me candidly that she's not sure what questions she's allowed to ask and that she doesn't want to appear stupid by saying the wrong thing. Well, if the committee has handled the recruitment and the orientation mechanisms in decent fashion with her, she has little to worry about. But just for good measure, use (say) a buddy system to help her through the newness. Ask your board chair to see to it that Ms. Adams is put on a committee or a task force or assigned to some board-level responsibility to make her feel at home. Trustee time is precious, especially at meetings. And you're entitled to the richness of the biases, prejudices, perspectives, opinions, intellect, and points of view of every single board member. It's obvious that evoking all of this from every trustee at the meeting depends almost entirely on the leadership skills of your board chair.

Mechanism IV: The Continuing Education Mechanism

Consider this: I'm one of your trustees and I'm impressed with my own intellect, with my skill at solving big problems, and with the high quality of my advice. So, if you keep bringing to the board table for *my exquisite* "judgment" ministerial matters such as approving routine compensation checks or computer lease renewals, or filling the potholes in the parking lot, or selecting the color of the paint for the hallways—if you do that, I shall be justified in feeling insulted that you consider that my role. Don't invite me back to the next meeting if that's what you want of me. And what's more, don't keep on sending in your senior staff to do dog-and-pony shows crowing about their triumphs over the last few months. I'm wise to that stuff. You do that because you want to (a) take up meeting time, (b) make everything look rosy, and (c) avoid controversy by having a smooth, uneventful meeting. After it's over, you breathe a sigh of relief and tell your spouse, "Well, we got through that one. Now I don't have to worry about another board meeting for a couple of months." The governance committee can't let that happen. I'm a sophisticated paranoid; I want to be part of the *real* action.

Let's face it, my continuing education isn't advanced by any of the above. Sure, I'd like a brief periodic oral or written report about what senior staff has done: It's part of my responsibility to keep abreast of that stuff. But my greater responsibility lies in being alerted to the big issues looming on the horizon—political, social, economic, societal—that are going to have an impact on my agency and for which we should be preparing. So make sure the governance committee has your support in seeing to it that our meeting agendas are enriched by you, our professional, leading us in a preview and review of those issues and how they should be handled at the board level.

Mechanism V: The Evaluation Mechanism

This is the toughest and potentially most embarrassing activity for the governance committee. It starts with a Lewis rule, and the rule goes like this: There is no such thing in our philosophy as the automatic renewal of a trustee's term. If my three-year term is about to expire and I haven't intentionally harmed, stolen from, or otherwise embarrassed the agency, the easiest course for the governance committee is to renew my term. That avoids having to go through the ordeal of a search for a replacement and all of the other activities to which I've referred in the first four mechanisms. As criteria for extension or renewal of a trustee's term, however, they're right at the top of the chain of stupidity. *Don't go along with it.* (I can't get out of my mind Reagan's response to the question of why he thought Meese was nonetheless an appropriate person to be attorney general. His response: "Well, he's never been convicted of a felony." Such an exquisite criterion!)

Before I can continue on the board, there must be a procedure for reviewing what I've done for the agency and how well I've done it; a procedure for determining my intentions as to continuing to apply my dedication and passion to the mission and goals. Prior service is not enough if the *quality* of that service is in question. There are many variations for these procedures, some formal and some informal. Just see to it that the board has one. You have the absolute right to the high-quality support from every single trustee. Get it? Well, get it!

Two final points about all of these mechanisms. First, the governance committee can figure out the details. I'm assuming that the committee has the ingenuity to do so, and I'm further assuming that you can help the committee in its efforts. I could make recommendations, I suppose (and here again, e-mail me if you wish—if I'm still alive, I'd be glad to help), but the mechanism in question should be related to the agency's culture and tradition, and you and the committee members know more about that than I ever could. Second, all of these mechanisms, if in force, can help to prevent the board meeting (Lesson 16a) from being the comedy of errors to which I've already referred.

LESSON 8—KNOWLEDGE FOR YOU TO PROVIDE TO YOUR BOARD

Five Important Areas

Your board will be able to provide you with the rational, consistent, high-quality support to which you're entitled only when it has the tools for making good decisions. I'm referring now to that exquisite moment during the board meeting when I, as a board member, am asked to vote "yea" or "nay" on a proposal on the agenda. It may be a proposal that you present for decision, or that someone on your staff, under your aegis, presents, or that comes to the board table as a committee recommendation. Here's what my approach should be. My decision—if it *is* to be rational, consistent, and of high quality—calls for my having access to five areas of knowledge. If put in the form of questions, they would call for the proponent being able to "defend" the proposal with reference to each of the five. No surprises here.

1. First, what is the *mission statement*? Learn every word of it. I probably know it well because of the orientation mechanism to which I've been exposed (Lesson 7). Then I view the proposal against the backdrop of the mission statement and ask myself if the proposal comports with the mission statement. The answer to this is what I call determinative, at least in one respect. If it does not comport, the vote is nay, there is no reason to consider the matter further. And now, coincidentally, I wonder how you and the board chair let it get this far if it's so out of whack with what we've declared for ourselves after spending all that time defining our mission (Lesson 1). If it does comport, then the tentative answer is yea, but we now have some more thinking to do, as you shall now see.

2. What are the *goals in the institutional plan*? This requires an assumption—that your agency actually has an institutional plan that clearly stipulates your goals. (Call them objectives or aims or what you will—you know what I mean.) Again, learn every one of them. As before, I probably know them well because of the aforesaid orientation mechanism. I then view the proposal against the backdrop of these goals and ask myself whether or not the proposal comports with each of the goals. This answer, too, is determinative. If it does not, the vote is nay. It's as simple as that. (Unless, of course, you and the board want to get into the

venomous nest of opening the goals "issue" before
we act on the proposal. Obviously, I don't recommend that at this time.) If it does comport, the
tentative answer is still yea.

Time Out: Before I go on to the next three areas of knowledge, I must point out that in the exercise up to now, we've
looked only at mission-related and goal-related matters
without regard to related questions such as budget limitations, staff limitations, and the like. Those considerations
can come later in the deliberations. At this point, we've
merely determined that it either is or is not *worthy* of further deliberations.

Now let's get back. Assuming that our proposal
passes the first two tests, there are three more
areas of knowledge to be considered. None of
these, however, is determinative. I mention
them only because I, as a serious-minded
trustee, want the knowledge (information) that
will help me make my decision and, equally important, make me feel more comfortable in having made it because I can now defend it.

3.   How does the proposal comport with the *agency's
tradition and culture*? If it does, that makes it easy
to vote yea. But if it does not, I might still like it.
After all, society changes, cultures change, and I
like the freedom of exercising my interpretive
privilege as a trustee. For example, as a matter of
chance, our home for runaway teenagers may
have accommodated only females for the first
seven years of operation. Now we're confronted
by Trustee Wilson's proposal to embark on a paral-
lel program for males. Our mission and goals
don't preclude this, so can we vote "yea"? Yeah!
We sure can.

4.   How does the proposal comport with the *trends in the delivery of like services*? After all, we're not the only safe house for runaway teens. Are the rest of those safe houses going in this direction? Just some of them? None of them? Even though I may be willing for us to go against the trend, I'd like the answers to those questions anyway. I can then feel justified in how I vote. (A word here about your role on this point, this fourth area of knowledge. If Trustee Wilson is the proponent, he'll probably rely on you, the agency's professional in the field, to do the research on these questions. That's quite proper.)

5.   How does the proposal comport with the *trends in society*? The principles of number 4 above apply here as well. How do we identify those trends? Well, we're all fairly intelligent, observant humans, and we all read and tune into radio and television programs. We can't help but know what varied and sometimes discouraging directions society is pursuing. And if necessary, you and your board chair might want to consider an occasional open discussion on just that theme. I recommend it.

LESSON 9—BE PROUD OF THE NONPROFIT TRADITION

The Beginnings of Nonprofits and Trustees

Let me tell you where and when all of this began. What I'm telling you is solely my theory, but it hasn't been seriously assailed yet. No, it wasn't Harvard College in 1643. Hell, that was just a few dawns back compared with the *real* beginning of the concept—the concept, incidentally, of both the nonprofit agency *and* the nonprofit board. The year was 268 B.C. and the place was India. The then-Emperor, Asoka (or Ashoka; it's spelled and pronounced both ways) had had his fill of successful and sometimes oppressive conquest and warrior-ing. In a moment of epiphany, he discovered Buddhism and embraced the concept of "dhamma." This meant "the good life," not in the sense of self-indulgence, but rather in the sense of devoting one's life to doing good for others. Certainly he, as a powerful emperor, was in a position to do just that. But unlike many emperors, he determined that that was what he *must* do, not just what he should *think about doing.*

He decided that he would identify the needs of his subjects in some order of priority, and then address them one by one, knowing that trying to address them all at once would probably lead to failure. His study showed that the single most critical need of his subjects was (imagine this!) universal health care, and he got right to work to remove all obstacles.

Time Out: The playwright in me forces me to confess to a scenario that goes through my mind at this point. Remembering President Clinton's many frustrations at putting in place a program of universal health care in our country, including Hillary's well-meaning intervention, I can just imagine Emperor Asoka, a consummate politician as well as a conqueror, bursting into the suite of the Empress and saying, "You stay out of this, I can handle it myself!"

In response to this obvious need, Asoka established 17 regional health care sites (clinics, really) and had them staffed by the best health care givers available. But even then, in those earliest days, there existed the caste system, and he knew that the staff—being of higher caste socially, economically, and culturally than the people they were to serve—would tend to operate the clinics more for their own convenience than for the convenience of the patient clientele. So in each region, he appointed representatives from the community to intervene and develop the policies and rules governing the clinics' functioning. He called them "dhamma ministers," and they were the forerunners of boards of trustees. Tell this story to your trustees some time. They'll love it.

But not only did Asoka's innovations in patient care set for all time the desirable structure for the nonprofit agency *and* its board, he also declared for all time the essential characteristics of altruism that should motivate both the agency *and* its board. Allowing a rough translation, he declared that the agency "shall render humane, compassionate and benevolent service to the community." More than two millennia later, this serves as an accurate description even today as to what the functioning of every nonprofit agency should be. But he went further. He declared that "it should be overseen by people of honesty and truthfulness." Here too, he created a description for even today as to the qualities required of a board of trustees. The words "honesty and truthfulness" must be interpreted in their broadest context: They must imply integrity and selflessness and dedication and generosity, and all the good things that we expect of people who are charged with the public trust. These were Emperor Asoka's proclamations in 268 B.C.[1]

Now, out of respect for something he forgot, here is *my* proclamation, which must be added to his: "And it must be administered by a competent executive and staff." That's Lewis, and the year is A.D. 2001. So there we have the agency, the board, and the staff. No different today than yesteryear.

Preview of coming attractions: Later on, in Lesson 29 (Chapter 6), I'm going to cover the issue of assessment, and

---

[1]R. Mookerjii, *Asoka,* (Delhi, India: Motila Banarsidass Publishers, 1995). S. Dhammika, *The Edits of King Asoka.* Kandy, (Sri Lanka: Buddhist Publication Society; 1993.)

particularly the matter of determining a nonprofit agency's "worthiness." When the matter of worthiness—worthiness of continued existence, continued community support, continued funding, and continued tax advantages—comes up with respect to *your* agency, you might suggest that the Asoka-Lewis criteria be used: (a) Is our agency rendering humane, compassionate, and benevolent service to the community? (b) Is our board made up of people of honesty and truthfulness? (c) Are we administered by a competent executive and staff?

If the answer to any one of those questions is "no," you've got a problem. Any reason to go more deeply than that?

LESSON 10—THE TRADITION SURVIVES, IN STRANGE PLACES

How about Palermo?

I'm thinking about the jumble of World War II, but stick with me on this because it really has to do with our subject. Later on, I'll cover the legalistic formalities that are usually involved in creating a nonprofit agency. But here I wish to make a point, a simple one, that the typical nonprofit agency is just a corporate form for carrying out *humane acts that are performed with no thought of personal gain to the actor.* In this case, I'm going to tell you about an individual, a former Army buddy of mine, Tommy, who was just such an *agency*, although not in corporate form. He had a last name too, but for now, that's not important.

In World War II, combat activities against the enemy were divided by geographical areas. In 1942, my unit was sent to North Africa after desert warfare training, and we were part of the Mediterranean Theatre of Operations. When it was all over, I began to think about the word "theatre" in the context of the popular form of entertainment known as "improv." That's the short form of "improvisation," we're told. Not all parts of the roles that we were called on to play in our costumes (then called "uniforms") were improvisational. In fact, many were prescribed—the uniforms themselves, the basic training, the immunizations, and all that sort of stuff. But once we entered one of those *theatres*, the improv mode became our role, and we had to do whatever the enemy's action called out to us to do in response. I take you now to August of 1943 to the once gorgeous city of Palermo, Sicily—and to Tommy's marvelously improvisational acts, none of them acts of war or combat, typifying what we in the nonprofit world are or should be.

Tommy and I met during basic training in Mississippi. He was a combination of elevator operator and street brawler from New York City's Yorkville area. We shipped out together to North Africa, did our bit against Rommel's Afrika Corps, then went on to the Allied invasion of Sicily. We drove the enemy out of that island in fewer than 39 days, mostly because it was defended by the Italians. Few of them had the will to oppose the Americans because most Italian soldiers seemed to have an uncle in Chicago or another relative elsewhere in the United States.

All was quiet in Palermo now, but it had suffered bombing and heavy artillery fire. The population was down to women and children, all of them hungry and many of them sick. All of them were trying to eke out a mere existence. My unit, resting there before our next campaign on the Italian mainland, was bivouacked in a large, partially crumbled villa in the center of the city. It had a large gated patio where the men were served their meals in their mess kits, filling the mess kits by passing through the chow line of serving vats that were set up in the patio. Soon the kids in the neighborhood, some very little, all raggedly dressed, came at mealtime. They gathered outside the gates and held out cups or bowls or just their bare hands, begging for the leftovers from the mess kits as the men finished eating. Frequently, some of the men would go with their food directly from the chow line to the kids' outstretched arms. Technically, this was a punishable crime, because the Italians were still then classified as "the enemy" and these were acts of fraternizing with the enemy. But even the higher-ups had to admit that these kids didn't seem like a threat to our war effort.

Tommy was emboldened by the situation—and deeply moved by the needs that he had observed. So he developed a plan. On occasion, he would follow the kids to their various homes and note the locations. Then, every few evenings, he would borrow my jeep with its small trailer, go to the quartermaster depot, and under the not-too-watchful eyes of the guards, fill up the vehicles with cases of food, blankets, towels, soap, and common medications. Then he would make his rounds to the homes of the kids and distribute the stuff there. This went on through the summer of 1943, until we were called to the next event.

I have made frequent trips back to Sicily over the years. And until quite recently, one could hear someone tell the wonderful legend of "Tomasso Natale"—the American soldier now known, with his Palermo-endowed new last name, as "Tommy Christmas." Tommy did not survive the war, but he does epitomize what a nonprofit agency should be. And I personally measure the worthiness of both the nonprofit agency *and* its trustees by Tommy's example: (a) what it does (they do) to alleviate a societal need, and (b) the selflessness with which it does (they do) it. You should, too.

CHAPTER 3

The Nitty Gritty of the ED's Job

Your job is a potpourri of unexpected moments—some comic, some semi-tragic, some fascinating, some boring—but all of them call out for your ingenuity. Some years ago, when I was preparing a Thai chicken dish for a family gathering, I needed dried ginger as my last ingredient but the stores were closed. Since the recipe called for soaking the ginger anyway, I used a cup of ginger ale instead and got rave reviews. Moral of the story? Simple—keep a bottle of ginger ale in your fridge.

LESSON 11—PLANNING

Do It, but Keep It in Its Place!

Every agency is going to be beset, both within and without, with the usual importuning about doing Planning. I'm capitalizing the word just this once because many of my scholar–practitioner colleagues treat the planning function as if it were a sacred rite. Get set for that attitude. No, I'm not demeaning the planning process, because there are realities involved. If you don't have *the plan,* you don't get *the funding.* If you don't have *the plan,* your mission could meander and so could your board and so could your staff. If you don't have *the plan,* you can lose all direction. I don't argue with any of that, so please remember that I've already said it.

But as I reach the threshold of my dotage, I have found that almost every declaratory sentence should be followed by a "however," and now I'm at the however stage with respect to planning. I accuse it of being frequently oversold, overfunded, overstaffed, and the subject of over-involvement. The planning committee of the board dominates the meetings with its frequent endless, breathless, precious interim reports. Staff time is gobbled up in support of that committee's voracious appetite for detail and support. What ought to be introspection on the part of the board tends to become inquisition, all to the despair of staff. Finally, the conduct of the programs and the delivery of the services start to get shorter shrift. If you're not careful, you go from the *process* of planning to the *business* of planning. And need I make the final rhetorical accusations? Yes, I must. Once you have the document, are you going to keep it in arm's reach at every board meeting thereafter so that the trustees will use it as a reference for its every action? Or will it just rest on some shelf? Well, kid, you know the rest of that thought.

One of my dear friends is the ED of a storefront-type, street-level community service agency. It counsels, refers, and deals on a daily basis with the social, financial, domestic, health care, safety, and housing concerns of the area's most needy, disadvantaged, and otherwise forgotten citizens. During a recent early morning visit there, I asked her what she and the board are doing about planning. Is there a plan? She showed me a copy of the "purpose" clause in her 12-year-old articles of incorporation, then invited me to sit in the storefront space for a few hours. Promptly at 8 A.M., the cavalcade began—cradle to grave problems (she called them "womb to tomb"), one after the other, increasing to a crescendo within a few hours. And so it went until 3 P.M., when she locked the door and hung out an old sign reading "Back at 4." She and I then brewed some coffee, and with a sigh, she told me that I had just witnessed her plan in action. "Nothing on the shelf here, Bob," she said.

What I just told you proves nothing, of course; it just illustrates something. Naturally, I don't recommend operating in aimless fashion or without some pretty firm idea as to the agency's direction. But my friend's operation was anything but aimless, and she knew damn well when she went there every morning what the agency's direction was going to be.

Okay, so where are we? *Yes*, I concede: You must insist that your board participate in, and give you time and resources for, the planning function. But, remember the following:

1. The plan should be a simple document with its three general and usual parts: (a) the mission statement, (b) a clear goal for each of the agency's functional areas—finances, facilities, staff development, board development, technology, marketing, public relations, networking, and strategic alliances (to mention a few of the scores of possible areas), and (c) the programs that will support the goals.

2. Recall Lesson 1: Don't fuss with the mission unless you've clearly outgrown it or determine that you must change it in significant measure. If it reasonably represents what you want to continue to do, leave it alone. Avoid, if you can, the

long meetings that deal with arguments over a coincidental adjective or two.

3.   Have a planning "task force." Don't call it a committee. "Committee" carries the overtones of permanence; "task force" implies that when you're done, you're done.

4.   Make it as small a group as is consistent with the idea of including major stakeholders. These days, almost everyone in the world can make some claim at being a stakeholder in a nonprofit agency, so use some discretion. Smaller groups work much more efficiently than larger groups. You know that. But be sure to have two trustees on the task force as well as yourself. And be further sure that you and they keep the whole board informed in writing, in intimate detail and on a regular basis, of the task force's hard work and progress and their own, and your, participation in it. Then the whole board feels "included" and—here's the big advantage of doing just that—this makes it more unlikely that the whole board will then spend too much time in overly detailed review.

5.   Limit the expanse of time and the number of meetings during which the task force will work toward producing a draft for the whole board's review and (eventual) approval. Anything beyond three months is unnecessary. Crowd the number of meetings if you have to.

6.   Arrange for formal adoption of the plan by the board. Include some ceremonial trappings. Distribute copies to all staff and, in your discretion, to some other "key" stakeholders, whoever they may be. Then, as I sneakily suggested above, have a copy of the plan at each place at the board table

for the next several meetings. That way, the trustees get to realize that it's the controlling document for agency functioning.

Experience tells me that the most difficult part of the planning process involves where it should start. Let's take the mystery out of that right away. I have my biases and I eagerly share them with you, and you, as the professional, are going to be the recipient of that first question: Where do we start? There's an easy answer that will set the process on a fast course. Once you have the task force in place, dedicate its first meeting to just plain brainstorming on one issue: *What are the goals that the plan should cover?* If you look at paragraph 1(c) above, I can explain.

For example, almost every nonprofit agency needs facilities of some sort. Okay, then, we ought to have the issue of facilities as one of our goals. This simply means that *with respect to the matter of facilities, we should articulate our aspirations, hopes, and dreams for what our facilities should be like within some identifiable period in the future.* And this same approach should be used with respect to every other goal that we want to include in our laundry list of dreams. Note: At this point in our deliberations, we are not going to deal with how that aspiration will be achieved. *That part of the plan will be considered by our staff professional (you), who will be charged with the leadership role of recommending and carrying out the programmatic activities designed to support the aspirations.*

If we follow that path, we shall soon have the meatiest part of our plan ready for the next step described above—the creation of the programs. If, of course, we're an already functioning organization, we might have some time advantage in the planning process. As an example of that situation, if we already have facilities, that issue jumps up right away as the subject of an aspiration. Let's be very specific.

If we're a hospital, we may want to express our goal for facilities as being the creation of a new nurse's residence sometime within the next three years. But at this point in the planning, we're not yet going to deal with the various steps—the feasibility study, the financial support, the selection of architects and builders, and the like—that must be taken to take to bring that hope to fruition.

If we're a membership organization, that issue too is likely to be the subject of a goal. We can simply express it as our hope to be able to increase membership enrollment by, say, 10 percent in each of three successive years. But at this point in the planning, we're not yet going to deal with the various steps—the public relations blurbs, the letters of solicitation, and the like—that must be taken to bring that hope to reality.

If we're a college, one of our goals may be to expand our student application "draw" area into another specifically designated region. We can so declare it. But at this point in the planning, we're not yet going to deal with the details of how that may be accomplished.

As to identifying other goals, we may simply have to use our imaginations as those goals relate to our mission and traditions and values. But remember—no programmatic steps in the goals section; just hopes. So once we, the board, have declared the goals, you will then be the focus of attention. The big onus on you will be to start creating the supportive steps (i.e., the programs) that will then be required to attain the goals. And underlying all of that will have to be a subset of our plan, called a development plan, that will (a) "cost out" the expenses of the programs and (b) specify the various fundraising efforts that will be launched and relied on to make it all come true. More about all of this, including the last point, in Lesson 12, which follows.

LESSON 12—LET'S JUST CALL IT "MONEY' (OR "RESOURCES" IF YOUR'RE SQUEAMISH)

Here's Your Board's Role in Fundraising, Like It or Not

The rule here is easy: There can be no successful fundraising effort unless the board—I'll give you your choice of phrases here—demands it or clamors for it or insists on it or takes ownership of it or becomes the corps of cheerleaders for it. *It must start and end with the board.* Your staff or your professional fundraiser will come up with a case statement to underlay and support the effort. But the case statement, the efforts of the director of development, the programs laid out by the professional fundraisers—these are all peripheral to the board's determination that it must succeed.

If you've been an ED for any length of time, you're going to hear the inevitable from some trustees. It's usually said pleadingly—"I'll do anything you say, but please don't expect me to ask for money." *There is only one allowable response to this condition: a resounding "no!"*

1.   The response that I suggest is the first of several rules that you and your board chair must impose with respect to the board's role in this worthy effort. It involves creating a *mindset* in every trustee at the very outset of his/her service or, even earlier, his/her recruitment for board membership. The mindset (and the rule) is simply this: There is an undeniable need for everyone in the leadership cohorts of the nonprofit agency to recognize the undeniable need for fundraising and the undeniable requirement for each such person to become part of the effort. Everyone *will* be "expected to ask for money." Period.

Digression: As you'll see a bit later in this lesson, we really may not insist that a particularly shy trustee actually go out

knocking on doors cold turkey. For him or her, we'll probably find some more appropriate role. But for the moment,
we want the mindset actually to "set" in, so that it really
becomes part of the trustee's consciousness. We can make
the adjustments later, but for now, no exceptions, no
Achilles' heel, no chink in our armor, no weakest link in
our chain. I could go on with those silly metaphors, and
I'm glad I don't have to. You'd be surprised at how quickly
that mindset takes hold. In the many consultancies that
I've conducted, the rule is usually accepted and embraced
just for the telling of it. Not because I'm the one who says
it, but because I remind the trustees of the importance of
their agency to the community it serves—that's what
brings them over.

2. Second rule: See to it that a development plan is in
    place. I referred to this briefly in the previous lesson.
    Now, even though this lesson is about fundraising,
    I'm going to use this second rule to illustrate exactly
    how the planning process actually works.

    • Our first meeting involves you and the board,
      and we start out by merely deciding the various
      areas in which we should have aspirations. At
      this meeting, we also designate the members of
      the planning task force (not a "committee"),
      making certain that it includes two trustees
      among its membership. We decide that we
      should do *something* about expanding member-
      ship, so the subject of expansion of member-
      ship is now identified as an area in which we
      would have a "goal."

    • Our next meeting involves you and the task
      force, and out of your deliberations on this
      issue, you develop the idea that we *should in-
      deed* expand membership. Eventually, it's deter-
      mined that membership should be expanded by
      increments of 10 percent over each of three

years beginning with the next calendar year. (This same process applies to each goal area, of course, but for the sake of simplicity, we're following this one goal area.)

- The next meeting—still you and the task force—involves a general brainstorming-type discussion of what range of programmatic activities (mailings, phone solicitations, etc.) should be considered as a means of achieving the desired result. This ends with the task force turning over to you the challenge of honing the various ideas into a rational set of steps (the programs) for going forward *and* the projected cost of those steps over the three-year effort.

- At the next meeting—still you and the task force—you report back, and the task force formally approves both the goal and the programs and arranges for presentation to the full board. (Meanwhile, of course, all of these various steps have been reported in painful detail to the full board on an interim basis by the two trustees who serve on the task force.)

- The full board meets and gives its formal approval to the plan and adopts it by unanimous vote.

Time Out: Please note that in this ideal scenario, we have achieved a plan in only two meetings of the board and three meetings of the task force. We have actually accomplished the planning, and we have actually kept it in its place. And now our last step in the procedure is the development plan. For this, we're going to take *all of the costs of all of the programs supporting all of the goals* and then decide on the entire package of fundraising activities that will yield us what we need—fees for services, annual fund campaigns, capital fund drives, foundation grants, bingo nights, silent auctions, and the like. (There's also the more exotic devices, such as "planned giving," which the cynics might say involve identifying people with terminal illnesses and helping them with their estate planning.) Now let's get on with the money thing. But one more important thought: At this point, the rest of what goes on with respect to this "money thing" should probably be put under the aegis of the board's financial committee or some equivalent board subdivision because we're now out of planning and into fundraising.

3.   Third rule: This is simple: Be sure your development plan comports completely with your stated mission and goals. When you go to the foundation to request its part of the needed funding, you'd better be able to prove that point.

4.   Fourth rule: Involve every trustee in both "giving" and "getting." Here again, when you approach that foundation, you had better be prepared to answer an honest "yes" to the question of whether or not every trustee has contributed in accordance with his or her respective means. Financial support is a *sine qua non* in the panoply of duties devolving on every trustee. That's the *giving* part. But we can't forget the *getting* part. As I've already noted, we can certainly understand the fear in the heart of the inherently shy trustee if we ask her to knock on doors cold turkey and ask for money for the agency. But there are other scenarios. Have her give you the names of five acquaintances who know of her affiliation with the agency, and *you* go with her on a planned visit to each. She's on your board because she believes in the mission and its importance to the community and she's made her contribution to it, and that's all she has to say. You can take it from there, fortified with your facts and figures and statistics and slick case

statement. And *voila!* Pretty soon, she's out doing it on her own. I've seen it happen.

5. Fifth rule: Make sure the board understands that the fundraising effort must *itself* be properly funded and staffed. Here again, your foundation will look for an answer to this issue. It doesn't like to fund fundraising efforts, as you can well understand. Your board must understand this, too. And as for you and your staff, you're not going to be excused from continuing to carry on with vigor and dedication the programs and activities that represent the soul of your organization and its *raison d'être*—okay?

6. Sixth rule: Keep the board continually informed of progress in the fundraising effort. Please remember that in respect to this activity, as with every other activity of the agency, the board has the monitoring accountability to the community. You can do this in concert with the board's financial committee, which we have now invited into the act.

But getting away from numbered rules for the moment, let's explore another dimension of fundraising. Rule 6 above might give you the impression that you're out there alone in front of the fundraising effort and that I, your trustee, am waiting passively for your report on results. This is an erroneous impression. Once again, here is where your leadership clicks in. For clarity, let's go back to a reference in Lesson 3, which lists the various areas of accountability/responsibility of your board of trustees—particularly the one that requires me and my colleagues on the board to "enhance the organization's public standing." This is probably the fuzziest and least understood of that list of 13 areas. Most of my trustee colleagues in the nonprofit world take this to mean, simply, that they must avoid scandal of such severity that it becomes the subject of an inquiring reporter's zeal. The meaning is vastly different. Let's go on to the next lesson.

LESSON 13—WORKING WITH FUNDERS AND OTHER CONSTITUENCIES

Playing It Smart

It's up to you now to set your trustees straight on this. And this applies to the board's role in working both (a) with funders and (b) with other constituencies.

Working with Funders

Take me aside and remind me (your trustee), if I have forgotten, that (a) furnishing the agency's resources is one of my basic areas of accountability, (b) my trustee colleagues and I have been selected because we personify the diversity that reflects the community that the agency serves, and (c) we are therefore responsible to interpret the community to the agency and, conversely, *interpret the agency to the community*—that all adds up to making sure the community knows what we're doing, why we're doing it, how well we're doing it, and why, therefore, we should be supported in our efforts.

As applied to the fundraising effort, it means that you're going to have to exploit the dignity of my position as trustee of a public trust, revitalize my passion for the agency and its mission, wind me up, and head me in the direction that I should be headed. First, have me make the initial contact with the proposed donor or funder—it's called "opening doors." That's not a casual phone call; it's a somewhat formal prearranged personal visit by me for the express purpose of arranging, in turn, a later and more focused, factually specific visit by you. My visit will emphasize my dedication to the agency and the reasons therefore, as well as my hope and expectation that my host will commit to the idea that the agency is worthy of support. If the cause is support for a particular program or fund, it'll be up to you to tell me what I should tell my host about it. Then, when it's your turn, take me by the hand, if necessary, and have me go with you on your visit to impress the donor or funder with the support for the issue at the board level and the importance of the effort to every member of that diverse board of ours with its matching community face. If follow-up communications are indicated, have me make them.

Board involvement is not only a component of the task, it's the *sine qua non* of the task.

I've referred in Lesson 11 to the development plan. This is the document that represents the job description for everyone in the agency who is in any way responsible for any aspect of the fundraising effort. Be sure to specify all of the above as part of the role to be fulfilled by your trustees.

Working with Other Constituencies

Use us. Use my trustee colleagues and me. Exploit us. Put us out front. Put us on stage at every possible occasion. Remember that when we sit at the board table, we "represent" the community, and that when we're in the public eye, we "represent" the agency and its diversity and its *importance to the community.* Each of us carries the dignity of the public trust and the onerous burden of fulfillment. Central casting may not think that we all look the part, but we stand for dignity, nobility, selflessness, and all of the principles of Emperor Asoka. Use one of us at one of your staff meetings; use one of us at your appearances at the Rotary Club, the Lions Club, and the local university. Direct us. Feed us some lines.

I'm honored to be here as one of the community's trustees, guardians, and supporters of (the agency), and to ensure that, under the direction of our ED (that's you!), it continues its noble task of rendering humane, compassionate, and benevolent service to the community. I serve on its board because of enlightened self-interest: Our agency improves and enhances life in the very community in which I live. Trustees, for the most part, stay behind the scenes. Their role is not always understood. Frequently, we are perceived as dispassionate, removed, and governing from on high. But that's not the way it is. We know the pangs of the agency and of the community. As trustees, we seldom make public appearances. I'm pleased, therefore, by this opportunity. The privilege of having some small role in the welfare of the agency makes me feel constrained to come before you and tell you how deeply I feel about its welfare.

It's up to you now. As with so many of your ED undertakings, you'll need the chair to be your ally on this.

LESSON 14—THE BOARD MAKES POLICY FOR THE AGENCY

Or Does it Really? Or, the Second Myth

Before I get into this one, I want you to know that I don't really *enjoy* exploding myths, because myths add so much to the romanticism in life. The Greek myths particularly, which I teach as another aspect of my life, inspire dreams that soar above the mere usual; imagination is not reigned in by reason. And it is so strange: The word "myth," which in ancient Athens had the meaning of "word" in the context of "*the* word, the uncontrovertible truth," has now taken on the meaning of pure falsity. I feel bad about that because the myths themselves are so deeply engrained in our culture. Our literature, our drama, and our art are all so replete with myths that I hate to think of them as common untruths. Let's digress on this for a bit, just for fun.

In the time of the classical era of ancient Athens, the world was young. And anyone walking through the forest would certainly see, peeping out from behind a tree, a naiad's face. Anyone kneeling down at a clear forest pool to drink would certainly see standing behind him or her in the reflection of the pool the figure of Artemis, goddess of the forest and of nature, standing over him/her to make certain the drinker did not despoil her precious forest or water courses. It's too bad that we can no longer think in those terms. Yet, as the world runs its course, we begin to be influenced away from unbridled imagination by a strange combination of cynicism and scientific analysis. Let me give you an example.

Take the case of Prometheus. This involved Zeus, king of the gods, who was offended by mankind (I use the term advisedly because women had not yet then been invented) and wanted to eradicate all humans from the face of the earth. Prometheus, on the other hand, liked humans and secretly (he thought he could hide the theft from Zeus) even stole fire from the forges of Mt. Etna and gave it to man to cook his food, light his torches, and warm his abode. Zeus found out about this act of disloyalty and decreed that Prometheus should be chained to a rock at the edge of the sea where, every day for 60,000 years, eagles would congregate and feast on his liver. Then, at night, he would be left in peace and his liver would heal, only to be prey for the birds when they returned the next day. At the end of that term, Prometheus was set free.

The ancient Athenians had no trouble accepting that story about the great hero, Prometheus. But things were different when it fell into the hands of people of science: They declared the myth to be pure folly. Sixty thousand years, they claimed, is too long a life even for a great hero and even under the best of conditions. And certainly, they declared, not even a hero could survive the infections that would be induced by the unclean beaks and talons of the predators eating at his liver. So now Prometheus is still myth, but under the new meaning. Later on, when we get to another myth about trusteeship, I'll tell you another myth. But for now, we're dealing with the assertion that the board "makes policy" for your agency.

The reality is that the board can't "make" anything for which it doesn't have the ingredients. Oh, yes, you've heard the tired old saw a thousand times. It's usually said in sing-song fashion: "The board makes policy and the staff carries it out." Bor-*ing*! But tell that old saw to a trustee and he'll nod his head in happy, resigned but uncertain agreement. He's uncertain, of course, because he probably doesn't know what "policy" means in the first place. Just so you yourself don't have that disadvantage, here's a good definition that you can pass on to your trustees as part of your educational program for them: *A policy is a statement of intent or direction designed to guide and influence all action by and within the agency at all organizational levels.*

A policy is the equivalent of a commandment, and you'll note that it is multidimensional. First, it is intended to exist for all time, until it is studiously and specifically changed by the governing authority (the board itself). Second, it applies to every cohort of the agency, top to bottom, left to right. That's why there are two "all's" in that definition—*all action,* and *all organizational levels.* It must therefore be drafted accordingly, so that not only does every (say) staff member know that it applies to him/her, but so every such person knows that it is to apply to that person's every decision and function.

Now that we're in agreement as to the role and definition of policy, let's see who "makes" it. I'll give away the mystery by telling you that, in reality, *you* do, even though in the end, the board will take credit for it. Here's the scenario.

An agency across town, similar to ours, is in the midst of a scandal. It has just been publicized in the media that the board vice chair has never disclosed his interest in the insurance agency that has been selling policies to the agency for the past seven years. At the next meeting of our board, one of the trustees, worried about what's happening across town, asks if we have a conflict of interest policy.

The comedy then begins. Someone then asks a more profound question: Do we have a policy manual at all? One of the elders thinks we do, but no one can seem to find it. Finally, it's determined that we don't have such a manual and that we're not even certain that what the board has enacted in the past can be regarded as being at the policy level anyway. Okay, we say, let's at least enact a conflict of interest policy, and the heads all nod in agreement. Okay, we say again, how do we do *that?* Simple! Note the many "*you's*" that emerge here.

I, as the board chair, say to *you,* "*You* know all about these things, Ms. ED. Please, by the next board meeting, get us some information about conflict of interest policies so we can consider what to do next." So *you* do the research, and at the next meeting, *you* brief us on it, even showing us some forms in common use for such a policy. We like them all, and ask *you* which one *you* would recommend for our adoption. In response, *you* pick out one, add a few embellishments based on *your* professional experience, and I then announce that the policy will be up for adoption at our next meeting. Stressing the importance of the action, I invite trustees who have any questions to direct them to *you.* At the next meeting, the board takes a vote (affirmative) and thereby "makes policy," just like a grown-up board is supposed to do. It then smiles in self-satisfaction.

But the great likelihood is that, unless prodded by *you,* no board would, *sua sponte* (that's a legalistic phrase meaning "of its own motion"), "make" a policy on the more esoteric matters such as diversity or strategic alliances or grievance procedures or sexual harassment or (heaven forbid!) board self-assessment. And just as a last thought—once a policy has been "made," the board is itself helpless to do more about it. It is still up to *you* to effect the articulation and the enforcement. This is true also as to the next myth.

LESSON 15—I'M THE BOARD AND YOU'RE THE STAFF

We're *Not* Partners! Or, the Third Myth

Of course, you'll hear the "partnership" rubbish a lot. In fact, a recent conference of a national organization dedicated to serving nonprofit boards was dedicated to the doctrine that we *are* partners. But, because I don't believe in preserving irrational myths (except for those that I teach in my inner-city community college course in Greek tragedy and mythology), I'm going to set you straight here. But not before I tell you another of my favorite Greek myths.

This, too, involves the mighty Zeus, but now in one of his more benign roles—not the oversexed, dissolute roue chasing around after attractive earthlings and taking advantage of them. In this myth, Zeus plays the role of patron of artists and artisans. He wants to encourage their attempts at bringing beauty into the world and plans to do so by creating personages to inspire them to greater artistic heights. So, he finds a willing mate, Mnemosyne, and mates with her nine separate times, all in one night, according to the myth. And the results of that union are the nine muses—of drama and poetry and astronomy and music and so on, all dedicated to beautifying life. How nice to leave that myth just where it is.

But it soon came under the scrutiny of the medical profession—the gynecologists and the urologists. They decided that the details of the mating scene were unrealistic. Then it came under the scrutiny of the gerontologists who, when they found out Zeus was 83,700 years old at the time, declared the feat impossible. Well, that certainly has taken some of the fun out of life for me.

But we must now get back to the subject, mustn't we? And that is the myth/untruth that you and I (and my colleagues)—ED and board—are partners.

A partnership is an association between/among two or more persons (or entities) in which *no one is subordinate to another.* Under that definition, you (as ED) and I (as board) cannot be "partners." It is patently untrue to say that we are, because as we look at our relative authority, you are definitely subordinate to me. I believe that it is said otherwise by some of my colleagues in the field so that we can have that unrealistic warm, fuzzy feeling that warm, fuzzy thinkers tend to want to attach to every human relationship. Obviously, it's nice if in our relationship we happen to like each other, but that's not a necessary condition precedent to our getting the things done that have to be done. Liking is no substitute for knowing our *respective,* as well as our *collective,* leadership roles in the affairs of the agency.

The fact, painful as it may be to you, my ED, is that you are subordinate to me. We've already mentioned (at least twice) that although your authority is "immediate," mine is "ultimate." Just as I had the authority to engage you, I have the authority to discharge you. You have no similar authority over me. And when you get into the grammar of comparatives and superlatives, "ultimate" is ultimate and there's no going beyond that in the world of words. It's not a marriage either, as some fuzzies like to profess, because we do not have the spousal declarations or, perhaps fortunately for you, the spousal obligations or privileges to deal with in reference to some repulsive board chair. However, some lamebrains refer to it as such in keeping with their warm, fuzzy philosophy. "It's like a marriage," the idiots say. (Do you get the impression that I think such ideas are stupid?)

If you really must try to put a label on it, just say that we're colleagues (Latin: *co-legare,* literally meaning *to delegate to two or more).* That's honest, and it implies that we're working together *at our respective levels* to achieve our mission. And it doesn't hide the fact of who has the upper hand. And if that takes away some of the fuzziness (and hence the sloppiness), well, it's about time you and I wake up to the reality.

But I too have some reality to wake up to. It is simply that even though I go around thinking that I'm the supreme imperial emperor and king in my agency, I mustn't forget that *you* are the one who gets things done. Because when I get finished declaring policy (see Lesson 13 above) or adopting a proposal that requires articulation to staff or the outside world or enforcement throughout the agency, you're the one who does all of that. So my supremacy doesn't mean much without you, my acknowledged "subordinate," doing all the things that then have to be done. As the lion said to Androcles, "Tell me, pray—who's *really* the boss?"

LESSON 16A—THE COMEDY OR TRAGEDY OF COMMITTEES

It's up to You (and Me)

The word "committee" is likely to evoke a smile on the face of everyone reading this. Theoretically, a committee is a handy little gadget for helping get things done in an efficient manner. A few of us on the board take over the task, along with supporting staff, of looking into a particular discreet matter confronting the agency and then bringing back to the board our recommendations as to its disposition. That way, 5 of us can concentrate on that particular situation while the other 18 of us are available to do other board-level things that you, the ED, require of us. That's the theory, and it sometimes works out that way. But, there's a "however" lurking in my sentence.

However (there it is!), the smile comes about when the listener remembers that the funny but worn-out old description of a camel is "a horse designed by a committee." In other words, those five trustees can quite likely make something complicated out of something simple just by virtue of the fact that they *are* a committee. It's true. They frequently take their task (and sometimes themselves) much too seriously. They regard whatever they're about as the most profound issue of the agency, consume lots of staff support time, and feel the urge to give interim reports of their progress on every occasion. Here are the six rules for undergirding a solid committee structure and functioning. I was inspired to try to develop them at the behest of one of my dearest friends in life, Dr. Thomas Horton— scholar, teacher, author, humanist, skydiver, and the holder of more doctorates in more fields than any other human. But most outstanding about him, aside from his obvious brilliance, is his sense of humor. If ever you have to take a 13-hour nonstop flight to the Orient, make certain you sit next to Tom Horton (I did once). The whole flight seemed to last about 20 minutes. He has a meaty comment on everything, and he told me his view of committees. It goes like this: He has traveled in every major city of every country in Europe and South America. And he has visited every park, plaza, public garden, and historical museum in every one of those cities. But he has yet to see a monument to a committee. (He recently informed me that in his travels in the People's Republic of China, he discovered, in a remote park, a monument to a committee. He is now revising his book.) Now back to my rules.

1.   A committee's role is to look into the board's concerns about a particular issue and eventually report back *to the board* the committee's findings and recommendation for *board* action. The *specific* committee's area of inquiry for making recommendations should be defined in the agency's code of regulations.

2.   The minutes of each meeting of the committee should be promptly prepared and distributed to each trustee as soon as possible after the commit-

tee's meeting. You yourself will probably have to see to it that this is done.

3. You are to use your benign conspiracy with the chair on this: Have those minutes include a message from the chair that each recipient is responsible for reading and studying those minutes for future reference.

4. The committee will *not*, I repeat *not*, make oral *interim or routine* reports at any meeting of the board. It will make its oral report and recommendation to the board only at the meeting of the board at which the board is scheduled to take action on the issue. The board is sufficiently informed on an interim basis by the committee minutes that have already been submitted—see number 2 above. This avoids a lot of droning-on, non-productive time at the board meeting itself.

5. If now is the occasion for the committee to report its recommendation for board action, help the board to make an appropriate response—one that doesn't go to either of the two extremes that we see so frequently. The first extreme is for the board to act as an automatic rubber stamp for the committee's recommendation. This is an abdication by the board of its responsibility for making the ultimate rational decision. The board should ask the committee to defend its recommendations with an explanation of the underlying facts and alternatives supporting its recommendation. The second extreme, however, would be for the board to get into too much minutiae as, in effect, to give the issue *de novo* consideration as if the committee had never functioned. The middle ground depends on a board whose members share a spirit of trust, confidence, and reliance in and with each other.

6. Some special thoughts about the executive committee. Almost every nonprofit board has one, and it's frequently made up of "insiders" such as chairs of standing committees, board officers, and the like. Further, the code of regulations usually provides something to the following effect: The executive committee shall have all of the authority and capacity of the board of trustees in the interval between board meetings (perhaps some few exceptions for merger, dissolution, and major acquisitions). I advise that you do what you can to see to it that this authority be used with discretion and as seldom as possible. You'll see what I mean when you get to the lesson on meetings, next up.

LESSON 16B—BORING BOARD MEETINGS ARE YOUR FAULT

How You and I Can Make Them Better, or the Next Myth

This is another long lesson, and it may be our most important one. I'll try to make it fun.

Let's get to the myth part first.

We'd like to believe that the board meeting is the occasion at which the intellectual, ethical, altruistic, dedicated, generous, and diverse elite of the community will gather to drop its pearls of wisdom. We'd like to believe that its deliberations will produce only noble thoughts on how to respond to the most profound issues facing the agency, and that pearls of wisdom will be dropping all over the place. Further, we'd like to believe that you and I, as ED and board chair, respectively, play our parts in harmony with each other. I'm going to use here my reference to my small talent as a musician, specifically as a bass violinist in a geriatric jazz group. I envision myself as conductor of the symphony orchestra known as the board of trustees and you as the concertmaster seeing to it that at least we're all in tune, with our musical scripts in front of us, and ready to play. I, on the other hand, must try to evoke from those players, once they're all in tune, every fine nuance of response—no unnecessary blaring from the trombone section, for example; ephemeral delicacy from the oboes; and gossamer tones from the clarinets.

That's the myth. Now we go to the reality. I think the best way of creating the reality is to present a realistic scenario, and we shall do so after this brief introduction. First, because committee functioning, and the rules by which they *should* function, are part of the larger process of board meetings themselves, I want you to review what we've presented in the preceding lesson. Second, I want you to add to that the following additional rules:

1. The agenda for the board meeting is the joint responsibility of you and me (if I'm your board chair). We must see to it that it is sent out to all trustees and that (a) it covers all of the items to be considered and/or decided at the board level on that occasion; (b) as to those particular items, it is accompanied by all supporting information, reports, and committee minutes not previously distributed; and (c) it includes all items for which you as ED need formal board approval, *as well as* some continuing education items representing the board's interest (e.g., long-term issues looming on the horizon on which you should be informing us and preparing us).

2. Don't let the board spend (waste?) time on minute, ministerial, or routine administrative matters. For example, some silly codes of regulations require board approval of all (!) expenditures. This is insanity when it comes to items such as routine compensation checks to staff, or renewal of a typewriter lease, or employment of minor staff. If these *are* necessary for board action, dump them all into a "consent" item on your

agenda and have them all "moved" and "seconded" and "voted on" as one item. (You might consult Robert's Rules of Order to learn what procedural items don't even require a "second." That could save some time.) And you might include in that consent agenda approval of minutes of earlier meetings. If anyone detects an error in the minutes or wants to clarify a conflict of interest issue, as examples, that particular item can then be handled separately.

3.   About the form of a board resolution, if required: If you and your chair can anticipate that a vote at the board table will require a formal resolution for on-the-spot consideration or adoption, the two of you should see to it that (at least) a draft of it is ready at the time. Nothing is more unproductive than to have the proponent of a resolution start to try to compose it *ad lib* and from scratch in the middle of a board meeting. Give him a running start. If it gets too complicated, have someone move to allow you and the chair to draft the final form of the resolution "in keeping with the spirit of the discussion." That usually works just fine.

Now, we're ready for our scenario. I'm your board chair and you're my ED. In keeping with our benign conspiracy, you call me up to talk about our next board meeting, and here's how the dialogue goes. I forewarn you that it gets a bit rocky at times.

Me: I'm glad you called. We have to talk about our last board meeting. Frankly speaking, I didn't like it very much. I thought that perhaps...

You: Please excuse the interruption, Robert. This conversation could well be called a *post mortem* (Latin for "after death") because to tell the truth, the meeting was deadly. All of the good discussion took place in the parking lot after the meeting was over. Why didn't that really good discussion happen around the board table?

Me: That's our fault, I guess—yours and mine.

You: Let's forget about fault. How can we make the next one better?

Me: That won't be hard. Anything would be better than the last one. Did you notice Susan Adams? This was her third bimonthly meeting since coming on the board. As usual, she sat in stony silence throughout the entire time.

You: Of course I noticed her. And I also noticed old Mr. Russo, now in his 27th year on the board. He just couldn't shut up. (Reader: Is this what we mean by the blaring of the trombone section?) I know he's our biggest donor, but that shouldn't give him the privilege of dominating every discussion. And while we're at it, I have to tell you that I noticed Jenny Jones, too. When we tried to discuss the contract for acceptance of the building—an issue clearly documented in the interim report of the facilities committee that I sent out with the agenda—she got that silly look on her face and asked, "What contract?"

Me: Yes, that was bad.

You (temperature rising): But there was something worse about that.

Me: What could be worse?

You: You accommodated her. You took the board's time by having the chair of the facilities committee go through the entire dossier of information that had already been sent to her by mail. And, by the way, that dossier was accompanied by your reminder and enjoinder that everyone must read those things *just so we don't have to go through that foolishness.*

Me: I guess you have the right to feel outraged about that. Just as I feel a bit outraged that *you* allowed Yolanda, *your* director of volunteers, to give her usual 25-minute report about her triumphs over the past two months. (I'm getting increasingly disturbed.) Doesn't she ever have anything negative to report? Anything in respect of which the board can be helpful? Anything about what challenges we're going to face with our volunteers over the next two years? Is nothing going to change? The financial situation? The political situation? The social situation? Is this just your way of keeping us massaged and relaxed and quiet?

You: Robert, this conversation of ours is getting a little more stressful than I expected, but it may be a good idea for us to have this out at this time. I have a few complaints, too.

Me: Good! Let's have them.

You: Well, you talk about *my* Yolanda. I'd like to mention *your* Mr. Covington IV. He sat there in obvious discomfort, using every conceivable twist and turn of body language to let us all know that he disapproved of everything we were doing. And finally he exploded with his favorite expletive: "Dammit, why don't we run this place like a business?" He's done that now three meetings in a row and no one has called him on it.

Me: I guess we both know who that "no one" should have been...me...right? Well, I guess that this calls for some thinking on our part.

You: I have one more complaint, but it's not about either one of us, it's about both. As I was going to my car after the meeting, I was approached by Bob

Taylor. He's been with the board for two years and is very devoted to our cause. He mentioned the report of the executive committee. He said that the report specified nine actions taken by the committee in the two months since the last board meeting. He considered each one of them as requiring significant policy-level decisions. He said that with all of that important stuff going on at the executive committee level, what need is there for his coming to board meetings just to learn what a minority of trustees has decided *for* him? He may resign from the board.

Okay, that's the scenario. You and I both know that our experience with each of these eight characters (I'm counting you and me in the group) represents an *endemic organizational problem.* But equally important, for each of the problems, there is a not-very-complicated solution that is almost totally dependent on how you and I, ED and board chair, understand our roles, particularly in keeping with our images as concertmistress and conductor, respectively.

So with this in mind, we can go to the endemic problems. It may be too late to handle the particular cast of characters whom we have already portrayed, but by facing some realities, we can probably prevent the same things happening again.

Susan Adams: We're going to make sure that we overcome her stony silence by working our magic with the *orientation mechanism* and the *engagement mechanism* (Lesson 7) administered by our committee on trustees.

Old Mr. Russo: I, as board chair (and symphony conductor), shall monitor and, as necessary, moderate his blaring so that his conduct at the meetings fits the culture of the board more harmoniously.

Jenny Jones: Here, too, I as board chair must diplomatically but emphatically remind her of her "pledge" to acquaint herself with all agency-related material sent out by you. I must, just as diplomatically, refuse to "review" on board time that which she has already received. Any such request by her will be ruled as "out of order."

Time Out: You see, in effect, the board chair is also the disciplinarian for the board, and you should use him or her as such when you need my intervention in a problem with any one of the trustees. Under no circumstances should it be necessary for you, alone, to go head-to-head in a controversy with a member of the board. Call your chair in on that right away.

Yolanda: This is your bag. You will see to it that from now on, the staff reports are concise, informational, and inclusive of not only the triumphs and the positive, but also the problems and the negatives. You yourself will then interpret these presentations to the board in terms of the future board-level study, discussion, and action that you want from your board.

Mr. Covington, IV: Shame on me! This is another blaring trombone. And to think I let it happen three meetings in a row!

Mr. Covington's question deserves a direct and rational answer, and I'm going to supply that answer in our very next lesson. It's a disturbing question that will confront every ED at one time or another. But it's almost always motivated in good faith, although it can sure raise hell at a meeting. I should have arranged for you, me, and Covington to have a luncheon at which we could have discussed the issue the very first time it arose—but I didn't. Now I shall do so.

CHAPTER 4

Board Relations

How's your sense of diplomacy? How skillful are you at euphemizing? And when necessary, how effective are you at staring people down? All of those questions are what are in the tarot cards in the hand that has been dealt to you. Before I was shipped overseas to North Africa in WW II I consulted with a Tarot reader who said that the cards suggested that I may not get back alive. I asked her to read further until she could tell me the "odds" on that word "may". After exhausting the remaining cards she told me "50-50". Considering that I'm still here, those weren't bad odds.

LESSON 17—DAMMIT! WHY DON'T WE RUN THIS PLACE LIKE A BUSINESS?

When Does the Nonprofit Organization Lose Its Soul?

Our home for runaway girls has gone through some difficult times, and the entire matter has now come for discussion at this meeting—the sudden, completely unpredictable

38 percent increase in clientele this month over the busiest month in our entire previous 12-year history; the need for increased referral people, counselors, beds, compartment partitions—you name it; and the unbudgeted $47,000 cost of all of that. What a challenge. So what about Covington?

Covington is a good egg; he enjoys being able to tell his industrialist pals that he's on the board of trustees of a home for runaway girls. But he doesn't like sitting through board meetings and hearing how we "waste money" (his words) putting up partitions in the dormitory so the girls can have some privacy. His well-meaningness is overcome by his business-oriented frustration and he explodes! ("Dammit, what privacy did they have at home?" He goes on, "And that $47,000 for the partitions was money that we never budgeted for." He rants still further, "I don't care that we had a sudden surge in demand for our services. Why don't *we* have to plan just like *I* have to plan in my department store business?" "You say we *do?*" "Have you ever thought of turning some of those girls away?" "Why not?" Then the punch line, "Dammit, why don't we run this place like a business?")

Covington is not alone, my friend. He may even be in the majority. Here's what I mean. If you want to face reality, you'll understand that nonprofit agencies like to attract to their boards people who are perceived in the community as having "made it." And of course, one of the most inarguable measures of "having made it" is success in business—success in the for-profit world. Covington comes from that world, and it's difficult for him to realize that most of the culture of that world has to be checked at the door when he comes to a board meeting of our agency. He needs an entirely different mindset, and it's going to be up to you, with help from your board chair, to explain to him what that entails. Essentially, it means that the cultures of the for-profit world and the nonprofit world are entirely different, and that the attributes of one are not the attributes of the other. But be careful. We're talking about attributes, not about morality or levels of altruism. We're talking about just *how and why they're different, and thus why they call for a different mindset* when Covington leaves his department store boardroom and comes to the board table of the home for runaway girls. We must not imply, and he must never infer from what we say, that his for-profit enterprise is somehow morally, or in any other way, "inferior" to our nonprofit enterprise. We want to make the point that they're just so damned different that they require different kinds of decisions at the different board tables. Let's get to some specifics. (Remember now, you and I are sitting him down in a comfortable chair and telling him, in the best way we know how, all that follows. Perhaps we can tie it in with the thought that someday, because of his obvious leadership ability, he may be the next board chair.)

The first point to be made is one that is the least difficult for him to understand. Here's what you'll be saying.

No, Mr. C. We're not suggesting that our agency shouldn't be following what you in the for-profit world consider sound business practices, like having financial records that can be audited, having job descriptions for staff, evaluating staff performance periodically, striving for efficiency so long as it doesn't impinge on the effectiveness of our service. But please realize, these are not practices that are indigenous solely to the for-profit enterprise. The business world has no patent on them. They belong in (and to) almost every agency of society's three recognized sectors—the government, the for-profit sector, and the nonprofit sector. But now listen to the rest of this.

If we're good communicators up to this point, Covington will now have quieted down. And when that happens, you can elaborate on the arsenal of differences between our two sectors—the for-profit and the nonprofit—so that someday he will realize that those two sectors *should not even be compared!* It's not like the nicety of comparing a clam to, say, an oyster. It's rather like the stupidity of comparing a clam to a breadbox or a locomotive. But people will continue to do so, so we'll have to continue to be part of that foolishness. So back to the session with Covington.

Distribution of Profits

If you want to get silly, you can start off by telling him that one of the attributes of the for-profit agency is that it distributes its excess funds (profits) back to its owners. Then, quickly remind him that if we in the nonprofit world did just that (considering that the board owns the agency, but only in trust for society), the recipients would end up in jail and the agency would lose its tax-free status and, further, lose its right to solicit funds tax-deductible to the donors. So let's get on with the other differences.

Mission

Another of the attributes of the for-profit agency is that *its sole purpose is just what the name implies—it functions solely to turn a profit.* Its mission is clear: We just stated it. The widget, whether product or service, by which it attempts to realize the profit is quite irrelevant. If the profit has been achieved, its mission has been accomplished; if not, it hasn't. By comparison, the nonprofit agency, although in general terms sharing with its sister agencies the requirement of serving some societal need, is required to have a specific, defined, and unique mission articulated by a specific, defined, and unique mission *statement.* It will stipulate what the agency is going to do and for whom, but always in its function of service to society.

Bottom Line

Related to the "profit" attribute is the criterion of the "bottom line" that pervades the for-profit world. Covington's publicly held business enterprise involves seven department stores in five cities, more than 3,000 employees, many thousands of shareholders, annual sales in excess of $2 billion, 600 different suppliers, and a yearly average of 66,000 customers per store. He also produces a slick 44-page annual report. But notwithstanding this complex apparatus, *the agreed-on measure of success of the enterprise can be found at the bottom of page 31 of the annual report. It's a single arithmetic number called the bottom line.* And in the for-profit world, success is *determined* quite simply. If that figure is "black," success has been achieved. If that figure is "red," success has *not* been achieved. And nothing else matters.

Well, you know already where we're going with this. The nonprofit agency has no simple arithmetic bottom line, so *that* can't be used as a measure of success of our home for runaway girls. There must be other criteria for determining our "worthiness," and we shall have to track them down in a subsequent lesson on assessment. The point to be made here is that we have to convince Covington to abandon the bottom line approach when he's on the nonprofit turf.

The closest thing we have to a (dare I use the term here?) bottom line in our agency, that is, the closest method we have of measuring success, lies in that two-element statement that constitutes our mission statement. Let's look at what we're doing and let's look as closely as we can at how well we're doing it—how "efficiently without impinging on our effectiveness," as I said above. Then let's measure against what the mission statement declares (a) what we're going to do, and (b) for whom. And there we'll have *some* answer to the measure of our success. It's as unscientific and imperfect as anything could be, but hell, we're dealing with desperate human needs, not widgets. And if our operating statement shows "red," that doesn't mean failure. Actually, it *could* mean that we're doing more than our share of (as Emperor Asoka stated) "rendering humane, compassionate, and benevolent service to the community." It could also mean that we're stretching out our resources beyond "prudent" limits. Well, Mr. C. surely won't like that, and maybe it can't last forever. But an operating deficit is not a necessary sign of failure in *our* altruistic world. Most nonprofit agencies realize less than 50 percent of their operating expenses from fees for services or admission charges or other sources of earnings on their own.

Listen up: I'm not advocating imprudence. I'm merely suggesting that the mindset of the nonprofit trustee must get away from the bottom-line syndrome. I repeat: Most nonprofit agencies that collect fees for their services earn somewhere between one-third and one-half of the cost of operations. So, "red" is not an unexpected color if grants and donations are slim that year or the "market" is unkind to the endowment. Enough about bottom line.

Board Profile/Stakeholders

But there's more. Let's call the first part of this board composition. Mr. C's department store board is made up mostly of "insiders," people who have some close affiliation or affinity with the operation of his enterprise (usually, you can find an actual business relationship). Here's a typical array: the president of his principal bank, a partner of the law firm that represents him, owners of a couple of his principal suppliers, and several of Covington's own high department store executives. And then there'll be a smattering of investment bankers, insurance company executives, and a few Covington types who are prominent in some other for-profit businesses or industries. Further, the for-profit agency has few—perhaps only two—sets of stakeholders. Primarily, there are the owners—the shareholders or partners or proprietors of the enterprise, all of whom are seeking the profits generated by the agency— and secondarily, but only peripherally, the customers. That's a lot different from the trend in profiles of the nonprofit agency. Because here is where we tend to start with an eye toward matching board membership with the profile of the community to be served. The board is supposed to be able to interpret to the agency that community, its needs and its trends and its attitudes; and conversely, it is supposed to be able to interpret to that community the functioning and relevance and worthiness of the agency. Obviously, diversity sneaks in here because most nonprofit agencies are created to serve needy and diverse populations. An aggregation of broad perspectives is therefore needed; a variety—a *real variety*—of points of view, biases, and strong opinions is a clear requirement at the board table these days. Thus, if this trend is to be respected, the traditional nonprofit board of the 1950s—(a) successful (this equates with wealth), (b) white, (c) business-oriented, (d) men— hardly fits now.

As for the open-ended definition of stakeholders with respect to the nonprofit agency, we can have some fun with this. It's difficult to determine anyone who *can't* claim to be a stakeholder. If we're looking at a university, for example, we're including students, parents, alumni, faculty, administration, the geographical community in which it has its campus, the general community within its academic reach, its accreditation agency, the graduate schools to which it will send its students with undergraduate degrees, the many categories of private donors, and the various government agencies that fund the myriad university's programs in financial aid and research and the like. You may be able to think of others.

This issue of profile/stakeholders quite naturally slips into thoughts about "stakeholder representation" on the board itself (I prefer to call it "constituency representation," so accommodate me by allowing us to use that term). So we're going to deal with that next.

LESSON 18—CONSTITUENCY REPRESENTATION ON A BOARD

Good or Bad?

As the pattern of diversity developed with respect to board membership, it brought with it some applications that had both good *and* bad results. You'll have to hearken back to the late 1960s and early 1970s of the last century. Changes in society were rampant—some motivated by good intentions, and some motivated by fear. The field of higher education felt the full blast of it. Students joined the other young people of the country in raising hell with "institutions" generally—not only those that actually functioned, like colleges and hospitals and social service agencies, but also those that were part of the culture of the day. No more formal weddings with clergy, no more senior proms, no more wearing of caps and gowns. Lots of incidents of students "occupying" the administration building—you can add to the list. That bothered a lot of us who were part of that newly despised class called "the establishment," but it also woke us up to some realities.

But no matter what the motivation, a great number of the agencies in society were forced to bust out of their traditional restraints. They began to believe, for example, that because the agency is a university, those (a) successful, (b) white, (c) business-oriented (d) men might be able to use a little help in their thinking about educational issues if they had the benefit of the *perspectives and points of view* of a smattering of students and even faculty, who were so much a part of the educational process itself. Such a liberating thought! And if we go back to the date of the founding of the early colleges such as Eton and Heidelberg, we realize that it took us almost 600 years to get to that point.

So more recently, many higher educational institutions provided for board membership—usually only one person each from those two categories—to attend board meetings and state their views on agenda items. Many state-supported institutions were mandated by law to make such arrangements, and this came dangerously close to constituency representation in its negative sense. As you can suspect, there's a universally accepted protocol that goes with board membership—one that I respect and endorse and support. In fact, I tell my classes that it's one of my rules, and here it is: There's no such thing as constituency representation on a board; decisions at the board table are to be made by those who can think *independently* on the issue, with no thought of self-interest or even the opportunity for suspicion that self-interest has entered into the process. By that, we mean that everyone who sits on the board may of course bring to the board table his/her (diverse) perspectives, points of view, and opinions—in fact, we *prefer* that not everyone think alike—so that in reaching decisions, we can avail ourselves of the richness of the variety of approaches that they bring with them. *However* (there we go again), it is incumbent on every board member to cast his/her vote in a way that "represents" the best interests of the agency as a whole, *not* the best interests of a *segment of the agency*. Yes, I know, I know. How do we crawl into the mind of a particular individual on this very subjective bit of decision making? If I "represent" the faculty at the board table, who's to say that if on the question of budget allocation I vote in favor of faculty salary increases as opposed to refurbishing the student union building, I'm *not* voting in "the best interests of the agency as a whole"? Tough, isn't it? Well, you see, we're not using as a criterion the inner workings of my mind. We're using as a criterion whether or not there is an opportunity for suspicion by any reasonable person that my self-interest has entered into my decision.

Well, there's a pretty good compromise available to us: Invite students and faculty to sit on the board as non-voting members. Have them opine to their hearts' content, then let the independent members make the decision after listening sincerely to all that's been expressed.

LESSON 19—DAMAGE CONTROL: TRUTH OR CONSEQUENCES

It's Your Choice

The term "damage control" has many innocent and positive aspects to it. It could apply to the salutary steps that are taken to prevent an unfortunate or tragic situation from becoming an outright disaster. Examples? Raising the height of the levee as the river water continues to rise, applying a tourniquet to the affected limb above the poisonous snake bite, or injecting the entire populace with the proper serum in time of a threatened epidemic. But thanks to our politicians, today the term has a serious negative context.

You know what I mean. It applies to the deceptions to which those in public life resort—usually in the form of just plain lies or baseless denials—when they try to avoid the civil, criminal, and public relations consequences of those previous deceptions that are now being discovered. Nixon and his cronies, including Henry Kissinger, accomplished damage control within the insidiously ingenious concept of "plausible deniability." This simply means that if you know in advance that some disgraceful act on your part might be discovered, make your plans now for how you might say that it didn't happen. Isn't it strange that admitting to such an act and facing the consequences would never enter their minds? (Here's an example of my hard-at-work tendency for creating scenarios. The scene is now the Oval Office: "You say that Cambodia's been bombed? Hmm, I wonder who it could have been. Could it have been the Guatemalans? Yeah, that's it. It's the Guatemalans!")

Well, ED, you may be surprised to learn that trusteeship has become such a sophisticated activity that boards are advised that, among the other policies that they enact, they should consider a policy of damage control. But to your relief, I must hasten to tell you that (a) if they have any common sense—and some few don't—they don't use the political model, and (b) when I advise them on the matter, the advice I give eschews any semblance of dishonesty and is founded solidly on *absolute truth and full and prompt voluntary disclosure. The burden is yours to see to it that this becomes the rule for your agency.* Have this understanding with the board chair before you accept the position of ED. Otherwise, the agency's taint that comes with deception or dishonesty becomes your professional taint for the rest of your professional life. I hasten to add further that if we discover the scandal before the public does, it's up to us to take action, which could very well involve you and the board chair making their own voluntary and preemptive public disclosure. Don't ever forget the doctrine of the public trust.

Sooner or later, something's going to happen. Your agency is going to experience the trauma of being at the center of a crisis. It may be a financial crisis (e.g., because of your rampant misprudence in your operations, you now find that you can't pay your bills, and the tragedy of having to close the place is looming on the horizon). Or it may be a programmatic crisis (e.g., those ten of thousands of foundation funds supporting your community theatre performances have produced nothing but a season of obviously worthless flops playing to empty houses). Or it may be a crisis of scandal (e.g., your board chair is publicly accused of accepting bribes to steer the organization's insurance business to a particular agency).

I realize of course that we are so anxious to retain our semi-saintly reputation in the community that we strongly wish that we could just deny that it happened and then hope that the world will continue on its inexorable orbit. No such luck! Oh, we may be tempted to deny it at first, just to give us time to decide how to handle the next phase of the situation...right? *No.*

We're going to handle it so that there's no necessity for a "next phase." The first and only phase is for us to admit whatever happened, investigate how we let it happen, and resolve to take steps to prevent it from happening again—whatever the "it" is.

There's a practical side to all of this. If we deny or dissemble or punt or fudge, we have not only shamed ourselves, but we have made ourselves fair game for the investigative reporters who suspect something less than truth. And you must admit that they, the professionals in their field, are better at the game of finding the truth than we, the amateurs, are at hiding it. But it's funny. In my experience with the handling of such situations, the aggression of reporters ends when we show respect for our obligation for assuming the mantle of the public trust by showing the respect for truth that is one of the essentials of that trust. If we answer the first questions straightforwardly, reporters prefer, then, to be helpful, not destructive. They're aware that nonprofit agencies fulfill serious community needs. Give them the truth, the facts, the data before they even ask for it. If they're publicly critical of you after that, so be it—it's probably because you deserve it anyway. We can then try to figure out how to avoid a repetition of the unfortunate event in the future, and the world will *then* continue on its orbit. Let's not compound the first offense of lying by being less than open with anyone in the community who has an inquiry.

So the first part of our policy on damage control—the nonprofit world version—is honesty, truth, candor, openness, or whatever you want to call it.

The second part is more logical than philosophic. It deals with the question of who within your agency will be the spokesperson in situations such as this. My experience has been that the first inquiries will be addressed to you, the ED. You supervise all of the agency's functioning and are the first to know all the facts. Also, you are probably more available to come to the phone than would be, for example, a trustee. But be forewarned: Reporter types are hot after a story that'll sell, and scandals are the best of all. They will tend to want to forage around among unwary trustees for some possibilities—they call them "leads." It's like the predator going after the easiest prey. Unfortunately, on many occasions, we hand them just what they need, *especially if we don't have a second part to our policy.*

Reporter: "Mr. Covington?"

Mr. Covington: "Yes."

Reporter: "You are on the board of Wayside House?"

Mr. Covington: "Yes."

Reporter: "What do you think of that scandalous situation in your agency?"

Mr. Covington: "What scandalous situation?" [Egad! We're sunk already!]

Reporter: "You know, of course, that your board chair is accused of accepting bribes?"

Mr. Covington: "No, I certainly do not. I haven't been to the last three board meetings so I'm not up to snuff on what's happening in the organization." [This is getting worse. The reporter now has an additional issue to pursue.]

Reporter: "Doesn't your board have a policy on required attendance at board meetings?"

Mr. Covington: "I have no idea. And if we did, I don't know if I could comply. You see, I'm on 17 other boards."

Reporter: "Well then, Mr. Covington, how do you keep up with all of your fiduciary responsibilities?"

Mr. Covington: "What is that supposed to mean?"

Reporter: "Your accountability to the community for a high level of dealings within your agency."

[Imagine. At this point, the reporter is telling the trustee about the public trust!]

Mr. Covington: "I just do what I can."

Reporter: "Do you know of anyone else on the board who might be able to tell me more about the situation?"

Mr. Covington: "Try Myrtle Finfgelt, the rock singer. She's the board's damn busybody."

Reporter: "Thanks for the lead, sir."

What's the result of this undisciplined lack of a second part to our policy? Merely this: Having caught you in the lie when you first denied the bribe story, the reporter is going to bring you still more deprecating attention with a new headline: Trustee Admits Ignorance of His Fiduciary Role. And it not so gradually gets worse. We wanted less of a negative image, but we're on the way to more of one.

So, quickly to the second part of our policy. I'll even give you some suggested language: The board chair (or some other designated member to whom you, the ED, will be in easy communication) shall be the sole spokesperson for the board of trustees. He/she will be responsible to respond on behalf of the board to all inquiries directed to the board level. All other members, when asked to respond publicly to board-level inquiries, will inform the person so inquiring as to this board policy. I tell you from tough experience, that although this cuts down on some of the fun that investigating reporters might otherwise enjoy, they respect the policy and will conform to it. And it is less likely that one bad move will spawn a second or third bad move.

It goes almost without saying that the designated spokesperson should arrange through you to become fully knowledgeable about the agency's affairs so that he/she can respond in an accurate and responsible manner when called on. And you—again, you—are going to see to it that that happens in just that way.

CHAPTER 5

Vision and Leadership

M ost of the material in this book is, of course, prose. But this chapter is more on the poetic level. When I lecture to my ED-to-be classes, I emphasize that the board should try to keep its energies directed at "the poetry of the nonprofit organization," meaning its mission, vision, values, aspirations, hopes, and dreams. The prose is at the level of roof leaks and parking lot repairs. Here's some more on that.

LESSON 20—VISION

What Is It and How Good Is It?

As the nonprofit world becomes ever more sophisticated, it also becomes a bit fancier. It's part of the unfortunate (in my opinion) tendency to take on some of the attributes of the for-profit world—logos, trademarks, slogans, and the like. In the course of time, then, we moved from having to have a mission statement to the point of having to answer (or so we imagine) to our funding sources if we don't have a "vision statement" as well. This, of course, brings out the worst in those of us who worship at the shrine that I call the "tyranny of adjectives." If we've been operating over the years, if we've been doing our thing, if we have a strategic plan that delineates our goals and our supporting programs, then we already know the *soul* of our agency. And I stand for the proposition that the word *soul* has so many overtones that it doesn't need definition. But nonetheless, there's a predominance of vocal "vision" advocates in our world.

For recreation, I sought out the dictionary definition of the word "vision." There were several definitions, but the one that relates most closely to the nonprofit agency is this ephemeral statement: "imaginary or prophetic sight beheld in sleep or ecstasy."[1]

That intrigues me. You see, I have attended and/or observed 3,087 board meetings in my career, and I must confess that some of the discussions and decision making seem indeed to have taken place while the trustees were in the dormant state of sleep. But I have yet to witness a board of trustees debate or reach decisions in a state equivalent to ecstasy. I must admit, somewhat ruefully, that trustees are usually incapable of such an extreme emotional reach, especially with respect to the issues that are on most meeting agendas.

Rather, departing from that ephemeral dictionary definition, the "vision" that I should like to see stated by your board is "an expression of the agency's hopes for its future benevolence in the life of the community." At best, this could be some qualitative community service that is notches above your present operational scale. This could represent a hopeful but studious balance between (a) its aspirations and (b) the realities of the resources that it can call on for the purpose—both human and financial.

---

[1]*Webster's Third New International Dictionary, Unabridged.* (New York:G. & C. Merriam Co. 1971).

In my professional life as a consultant to nonprofit agencies, the "vision" thing comes up frequently, and it always gives me a chuckle because vision has such a different personal meaning for me. In the sense of visual acuity (actual eyesight), vision has been a chronic problem with me ever since puberty, when I was damned not only with those usual ghastly physical changes that a boy experiences, but also with a case of near-sightedness highlighted by 20/600 vision in my left eye. This became a serious problem for me in the dark days immediately after Pearl Harbor, when the Navy and the Marine Corps both fell into paroxysms of laughter as I, in trying to offer my pitiable body to the war effort, came to the station in the physical examination when I was ordered to read the eye chart. I should like to attribute their laughter to my catastrophic performance during the eye chart incident, although I must confess that I was standing there only in my underwear, as well.

But, still filled with patriotism, I decided that my last chance was the Army. And by this time, by careful observation, I had learned something about the mystique of hastily conducted physical examinations. The medical officer administering the eye examinations at both the Navy and the Marine recruiting offices worked rather quickly and sometimes carelessly in order to process the scores of scantily clothed, shivering volunteers lined up one behind the other on those cold December days in 1941. And they all followed a standard routine: "Cover your left eye and read with your right eye; that's fine. Now cover your right eye and read with your left eye."

Sure enough, as I hoped would be the case, the medical officer at the Army recruiting station followed the same procedure. In due course, I approached the chart, covered my left eye with my left hand and, with my fairly good right eye, read the chart with sufficient accuracy. And when he said, just as I expected, "That's fine, now cover your right eye and read with your left eye." I took advantage of his lack of concentration, changed hands (not eyes), read the chart again with my right eye, passed my physical, and achieved the exalted status of private in the U.S. Army. The reward was $21 per month, room and board, itchy uniforms, lots of inoculations, and learning how to respond "yes, sir" to every inconceivable command. (I'm glad to tell you that after four years, I had advanced to the rank of a junior officer, at which point the monthly pay was about $127 and the uniforms were less itchy.)

There was a terrible irony in this deception of mine as to my vision, however, and a bit of poetic justice for my dissembling. The Army, impressed with my visual acuity, assigned me to be a forward observer in an artillery combat unit scheduled for transshipment to North Africa. And there, thick glasses and all, I personally became part of our country's first line of defense against General Rommel and his dreaded Afrika Corps.

So much for vision.

It could get worse. There's another topic on which some agencies find the opportunity to allocate too much time; it's called a "statement of values." How fancy can we get? If we've got a good mission statement and a solid institutional plan, our values should be quite visible to anyone who takes the time to care. Don't go down that primrose path.

LESSON 21—LEADERSHIP AS A CONCEPT

What Is It? Can it Be Taught?

In the quadrillion books and articles and speeches about, and emerging from, the nonprofit world, the word "leadership" is bandied about as if it had a commonly agreed-on meaning. It doesn't. And now, after my having achieved octogenarian status, I still strain after its real meaning. Don't bother looking in the dictionary—that merely leads you around into an endless cycle of nothingness. You know the deal: First you'll be told that leadership means the quality of being a leader. Then you'll be told that a leader is one who leads. It's all so silly that I haven't even bothered to use quotation marks in those last two sentences. I'm therefore concluding that the word leadership has no clarifying definition, and that its real sense emanates from identifying the qualities of one whom we recognize as a leader. I'm going to use my own standards. I've thought a lot about how to *describe* a leader, because not even Webster can help me define one. Here's how I'd distinguish a leader from the rest of the crowd; it's one who has (a) a compulsion or a desire to achieve a certain result, (b) the determination to continue the effort until the result is achieved, and (c) the willingness to assume the attendant risks.

I chuckle when I think of the term leadership—the qualities of being a leader as I have conceived them—being applied to many of the trustees who populate the nonprofit world that *I know.* I wish it were otherwise, but the reality sets in when I see so many of them who don't even take the trouble to get to meetings on time! Quite a display of (a) desire, (b) determination, and (c) willingness to assume risks, isn't it? I know that I'm letting my cynicism show through, but that's why I'm writing this book. I simply must enlist you in the ranks of those of us who truly believe that trusteeship calls for something a lot more than an interest in the agency that is merely casual or sporadic or dilettantish or *ad hoc.* It calls for—let's say it—*leadership.*

And before I leave the subject, I want to propose the unpopular idea that leadership cannot be *taught.* I sneer at the various programs of so-called "leadership training" for the simple reason that desire, determination, and willingness to assume risks cannot be taught. You'll see those vacuous programs in every community. Some screwball got the idea that you can make a leader out of a person by exposing him or her to the community's executives in business and the professions, in industry and banking and politics and other areas of "influence and power." In many instances of which I am aware of, the process involves using as role models people in power without any necessary regard to how they use their power. It smacks of the idea that to "get things done," you need only go to the right places and the right people. That's not leadership. You're either a leader or you're not.

I equate the situation with the other two statuses that, I believe, cannot be taught. First, I strongly believe that one cannot be taught to be a teacher. I'm not referring to the ministerial moves of taking attendance and grading papers. I'm referring to a quality of being able to communicate from your soul to the soul of another. Who can teach you that?

Second, I believe equally strongly that one cannot be taught to be a comedian. You either are one or you're not—that depends on some mysterious *je ne sais quoi* quality conferred on one by some deity, probably Dionysus, the god of wine. There are many comics in the world, of course, but few comedians. My late brother was one of the few, and he was one of the best. He never told jokes or wore funny hats. He'd just come in to a room, smile at everyone present, then in the course of conversation he'd emit a discreet giggle. And within moments, everyone in the room was looking at him and roaring with laughter.

Well, so much for that aspect of leadership. There's more.

LESSON 22—LEADERSHIP: THE USUAL BOARD/ED KIND

This Is Merely an Algebraic Equation

Way back in the introduction to this book, I referred to the leadership component of your agency as being composed of two elements—the board and the staff. I then defined the respective areas of their leadership roles by simply noting that one is charged with "governance" and the other is charged with "management." This is one way of expressing what is an oversimplification. The fact is, and experience dictates, that the so-called respective charges are not always identifiably respective; they converge and join on occasion, diverge on other occasions. Later on, in Lesson 23, I'm going to explode in more detail the myth that there's a *clear* delineation between areas of governance and areas of management—that you and I can know with precision exactly what issue is going to be decided by exactly which element of leadership. But for now, I'm going to deal with why, with respect to some *particular* issue, leadership in one organization may take a form that is vastly different from leadership in any other. My answer to that "why" is that it's the result of the dynamics of human interaction within that particular organization. I construct this equation as follows:

Rules x Personalities = Operational Protocols

Our scenario again: I'm the chair and you're the ED. With respect to a particular *rule*, our mix of personalities will interact and create the *protocol* by which that rule will be carried out. So be prepared to take a tolerant approach to the idea that although rules may be standard for all nonprofit agencies, protocols under which the rules are effectuated are under constant change, and personalities that drive those protocols are so diverse as to make the protocols unpredictable.

For example, let's use a rule from one of the dozen or so areas of accountability of the board of trustees listed in Exhibit 1–1. The third on the list requires that the board—that's me for this example—periodically evaluate and assess your performance as ED. That's the rule under consideration. But how this is actually carried out between us will depend to a great extent on the chemistry of our two personalities—yours and mine. And how we do it may be in some agreement with, or perhaps in sharp contradistinction with, how it is done in any (or every) other agency in the nonprofit world. Each mechanism in each such agency will (again) depend almost entirely on the *chemistry* of the personalities of the specific human beings who comprise its leadership component—the you's and me's of each.

As an example of the example, assume this situation: Our board is made up of the usual successful business-men types—bottom-line people, they call themselves. They know that I'm one of them in all respects, and that as well-meaning humanoids of that ilk, we all still believe that we have to "run this place like a business." So it's

- just the facts, please

- give them to me fast

- we're all busy men, you know

- we don't need a lot of unnecessary discussion

Added to that is the fact that I'm a dominant and domineering guy and you don't have the self assurance to contend against me. (Remember, this is just a scenario. But it's what we're dealing with in this example.)

You politely remind me that it's time for your biannual evaluation.

Board chair: "It is?"

Executive director: "Yes."

Board chair: "What do you suggest I do?"

Executive director: "Most boards would appoint a committee to review my performance against, say, my job description and the goals in our strategic plan. I'll help with that if you wish. Or you might even ask me to do a written self-evaluation to start the process."

Board chair: "That means more meetings and such, right?"

Executive director: "Probably so."

Board chair: "Well, ED, I have a better idea, and it's a lot simpler and quicker. I'll get the guys together and ask them one question: 'How well are things going around here?' If the answer is, 'They're going well,' I'll adjourn the meeting and you and I will discuss a compensation increase. If the answer is 'They're not going well,' I'll ask for your resignation. How does that grab you?"

Somehow, I detect in the background noise to this statement the braying of a jackass. But nonetheless, for our agency at that time in its history—and with those particular personnel in the leadership role—that becomes the protocol by which that particular rule is enforced. And in a similar manner, all agencies develop an aggregation of protocols that then become the agency's culture. Yet, change a personality or two within the leadership mix, and we have a vastly different protocol for the same rule.

In the example of our agency and you and me, let's assume that the years have brought some changes in the personality element of our equation. I, and several others of my bottom-line admirers/clones, have been replaced by a much more diverse group of successors. You, the previously (and understandably) cowed ED, feel increasingly comfortable with the new chemistry and are somewhat emboldened. Things have been going well, the trustees have turned to you more frequently for your guidance and advice, and they clearly understand and respect your share of leadership and the necessity for it. In fact, the new board chair reminds *you* that it's assessment time, and you respond with your agreement that it *is* time. But now, with your new sense of self-assurance, you impose some conditions. You strongly suggest (that's my euphemism for insist) that the review be based on some mutually agreed-on, measurable criteria and a previously agreed-on mechanism for the process. And when the chair asks for specifics

1.   as to the measurable criteria, you refer him to (a) your job description, (b) the provisions in your code of regulations describing the ED's areas of functioning and authority, and (c) the goals delineated in your strategic plan, all three of which may specify or at least imply what's expected of you;

2.   as to a previously agreed-on mechanism, you'll remind him that your employment agreement specifies the details of not only the above criteria, but also that they would be applied by a small *ad hoc* board committee that would also consider the effectiveness of the board's *own role in supporting, advising, and encouraging the ED*, as required by the second area of accountability set forth in the board's job description referred to in Lesson 3 in this work. Thus, your board, now less impatient with process and a lot less bottom-line oriented, agrees. And the culture of your agency is now in re-formation because of the new protocol. In one lesson, you see, I have illustrated two different protocols for the same rule. And note further that, in our scenario, it happened in the same agency, but at different times.

One more thought: One of my "no such thing" Lewis rules is this: There is no such thing as the unilateral assessment of the ED's performance. It necessarily involves considering the board's performance as well. The board cannot stand innocently by with the attitude of let's see how well *you* performed as an ED without regard to how *we* performed as a board. Any questions? Just let me know.

Wait a minute. I have still another thought, and it's about your compensation. The two issues of (a) your review and (b) your compensation should be recognized as two semi-separate issues. For example, if there is a "norm" for the compensation level for an ED in your agency's line of effort, at your agency's particular size, and in your agency's geographic area, your compensation should not go below that norm as long as your assessment concludes that you are performing at least "satisfactorily" and are therefore worthy of being retained in your position. That's the first step in the review. The second step involves how far above "satisfactory" level you have performed and to what extent that should translate into an increase. If you are *fairly* judged to have performed below the "satisfactory" level, the norm should not be reduced—you should simply not be retained.

LESSON 23—THERE'S A CLEAR DISTINCTION BETWEEN GOVERNANCE AND MANAGEMENT

Or Is There? (That's the Fifth Myth)

This is the last of our five myths about nonprofit leadership. Stay away from some of those seminars to which you'll be invited, particularly those that propose a neat line of authority between you and me. In Lesson 13, I discussed "policy" in the context of the tired old saw that states that "the board makes policy and the staff carries it out." Now, we're going back to the topic of policy for another purpose. We're going to equate a few terms in the context of *turf*.

Time Out: The reality is that the board and staff disagree on turf issues more frequently than agree. They contend with each other at times, and cause each other stress and anxiety when they try to figure out which of them has the authority to handle which particular problem or to answer which particular question. That warm, fuzzy feeling that our nonprofit colleagues like to attribute to us just isn't there. Let's face it. I've heard it all from staff a thousand times and so have you: "Why is the board interfering in management issues again?" Or, by way of contradiction: "Those decisions from up here on high—why don't they meet with *us* to discuss these things?" As we go further into this, we'll look at examples.

Table 5–1 shows the traditional division of turf between you and me, using the traditional terminology.

Neat, isn't it? Sure it is—at least as a series of columns. But how about the application as to a particular issue: Is it a "policy or governance matter" (my jurisdiction) or an "administration or management matter" (your jurisdiction)? In truth, you may not be able to tell merely by reference to that columnar stuff. Sometimes, of course, you can. For example, on the face of it, if you're the president (ED) of the university and the issue is whose turf it is to employ subordinate staff, that's clearly your turf. Right? Right! Or if you're the ED of a ballet company and the issue is the color of the tutus that the ladies of the company will wear in the next production, that too is your turf (although you'll probably delegate that seemingly micromatter to the artistic director if you have one). Right? Right! But then come the complications. So I'm suggesting that we use an admittedly less precise set of columns, but it's a lot more fun to use, and I like it because it has a literary bent to it. (I forewarn you that it presupposes that we have an institutional

Table 5–1 Traditional Division of Turf between Board Chair (Me) and Executive Director (You)

My Turf	*Your Turf*
Policies of the agency	Administration of the policies
Governance of the agency	Management of the agency
Accountability for the agency	Responsibility for the agency's functioning

plan or call it what you will—strategic plan, as an example—that clearly states our mission and our goals. If we don't, my only comment is: Shame on all of us.) So now, with our plan in place, let's look at this columnar presentation (Table 5–2) instead.

Here's why I like *this* columnar arrangement better. Under the previous columnar arrangement, a particular issue that masquerades as "administration" (your turf) can really be "policy" (my turf), depending on either (a) the time in the life of the agency when it arises, or (b) some unusual outside factor. As an example, assume that the university of which you are the president seeks a professor of poetry. There is no question but that you, as chief executive officer of the agency, should not have to seek board action with respect to the hiring of faculty or any subordinate staff. But get ready now for the next "however."

However (see, I warned you), it is 1939, and you, as a literary purist, have decided to offer the position to Ezra Pound, a brilliant poet by any standards. Yet, as the world knows, he is an expatriate American living in Italy, a strong supporter of Mussolini and Fascism, an outspoken anti-

Table 5–2 The "Lewis" Version of the Division of Turf

My Turf	*Your Turf*
Mission-related issues	Goal-related issues (we share this)
Goal-related issues	Program related issues
	OR
The "poetry" of the agency—its aspirations, hopes, dreams and values	The "prose" of the agency—the programmatic activities designed to achieve my poetic goals

Semite, and one who frequently broadcasts seditious radio messages back to the United States. Well, clearly, under the first set of columns, the decision is inarguably yours because it comes precisely under "management of the agency." If that's the set we use, you and I (I'm your board, remember) can get into a pretty hot controversy when I try to intervene because of what I consider "some unusual outside factor." As to the turf issue under *that* set of columns, I simply can't win.

But if we go to the other set of columns, I can conscientiously prevail and, conversely, you can't conscientiously get your nose out of joint. I'll just use either of two arguments. First, I'll contend that with respect to the "aspirations, hopes, dreams, and values" of the university, the selection of Ezra Pound would be an unwise choice. Second, I'll contend that in view of the storm clouds of war against Nazi and Fascist powers facing our nation, our very reputation as a university would be challenged by students, alumni, funding sources, and the community at large—all of those elements interfering with our attainment of mission. Yes, I know, a university is supposed to be a fortress for free speech and the free exchange of ideas, but this is one instance in which bad timing—I experienced that era—could have brought down the entire university.

A personal reminiscence about Ezra Pound. In 1939, he was invited back by the faculty of little Hamilton College, my *alma mater,* to receive an honorary degree for his achievements in poetry. I was a reporter for the college paper and was assigned to interview him. Knowing his reputation as an *enfante terrible*, I was quite intimidated by the task. But he was gentle and kind and tried to help me in every way in my need for writing a good article. I never forgot that. And in 1945, after Pound had been captured and taken by U.S. troops as a prisoner of war and sent to the Army Disciplinary Training Center outside of Pisa, Italy, I visited him there briefly. I was a lieutenant at the time and wanted to return the favor of six years before, just by show-ing a bit of friendship. Although thought by many to be "mad," he greeted me warmly, claimed—probably falsely—to remember me from the Hamilton College interview, and embraced me when I left. But back now to our issue.

The same logic that we used in the Ezra Pound example can be applied to the "tutu" situation. We'll change it a bit. Now, instead of you (or your artistic director) deciding that the tutus should be blue, you decide that there should be no tutus at all—that the ladies shall dance in the nude. Here again, under the first set of columns, I don't have a right to intervene. But in the second, I have a clear right to do just that and to overrule your judgment. You know what I mean—values, community standards, funding sources, and all that sort of stuff that a board has to be concerned about. Wanna fight about that?

Two more points. First, we've used the terms "responsi-bility" and "accountability"—the first applying to you and the second applying to me. Here are the meanings that I like to attribute to them. "Responsibility" is your obligation with respect to the *performance* of a particular agency func-tion. "Accountability" is my obligation to *monitor that per-formance and see to it that it supports the attainment of our mission and goals.*

Second point. Let's go back to the first set of columns for purposes of making this point. "Turf," you'll see, is a never-ending issue between you and me even when we think we've got it right. Let's assume that we've worked so well together for so many years that we never have a con-troversy as to who attends to which matter. I have every confidence in you, and when it comes to a particular issue within the realm of your "responsibility," I stay out of the way. I "know my place." In other words, we have devel-oped a perfect entente between us. We know the difference between governance and management, and I rule over the former and you rule over the latter. As to each other, that's our job description. But here's where the entente breaks down. You, my ED, get involved in a programmatic or financial or personal scandal. You do something "creative," like putting imaginary people on the payroll or using agency funds to pay your personal home mortgage. The world finds out about it and the editorials scream out, "Where was the board during all of this?" Well, based on our entente, I suppose I could answer something to the effect that I'm in governance, not management, and that I can't be expected to look over my ED's shoulder every moment, and that there's a rule that I should never get into micromanagement. Right? *Wrong!* The nice cozy entente between you and me may be binding on us, but it isn't binding on the community, the funding sources, our stakeholders, the Internal Revenue Service, or the world at large. And as far as those folks are concerned, that rule is a silly nullity.

A closing thought about this policy thing. "Policy," as a concept, exists at every level of agency functioning. A "macro" board policy will spawn "micro" policies up and down within the agency. So that when I proclaim a governance "policy" of cost control and austerity, you will proclaim a management "policy" of turning off unneeded lights and air conditioners as rooms are vacated for the night.

CHAPTER 6

Looking Ahead

T here are warnings throughout this book about the difficulty of being an ED. It will only get worse, so "screw your courage into place." And note well: This is *Lady* Macbeth saying this. And she didn't even have to educate a board of trustees, or staff its committees, or remind the board of its required level of accountability, or deal with an irascible chairman or disobedient staff members, or resolve a financial crisis or a programmatic crisis or a crisis of scandal, or.......Need I go on?

LESSON 24—THE 20TH CENTURY

Tough Time for the Nonprofit World

I used the word "tough" in the title to this lesson. It's also a tough lesson to articulate, and it leads into a series of tough lessons that follow. Here's the pattern, in outline form, of what we'll be doing.

1. *Source of the tough time*—explosive growth in the number of nonprofit agencies

2. *Traumatic change in the nonprofit world's environment*—competition for survival

3. *Our responsive actions in the new environment*—attention to

- marketing and program delivery

- public relations

- consumerism

- stakeholders

- diversity

- assessment

- strategic alliances

Let me start this out with a personal disclaimer: I lived 80 years of my life in the 20th century and I have no illusion about it being "the good old days." On the whole, it was one of the most trying and violent centuries in the entire history of the world. Throughout the 1900s, we experienced the hopelessness and deprivation of the Great Depression ("great" here has no positive meaning at all), and our citizens fought in four great (there's that word again) wars, not counting Desert Storm. In the Depression, my family, like many others, drank grade B milk, and our diet included a lot of bread pudding and gelatin, and several of my family members sold apples on the streets of New York. As to the wars, I spent four years in military service in World War II—North Africa, Sicily, Italy, and Southern France—and to this day, the two ounces of German shrapnel still ensconced in my left buttock set off the alarm as I go through the security devices at the airports (very embarrassing). I have no illusion about it being a wonderful era for humankind. But except for one aspect in the life of nonprofits—explosive growth in their numbers (the cause of most of their resultant turmoil)—it could have been a golden era for them. As it happened, it wasn't.

A survey of the changes confronting the nonprofit leadership corps from, say, A.D. 1901 to A.D. 2000, can blow the average mind. Some were (let's use the term) "good," and some were not so good. Some actually make me grieve, as you'll see somewhere in the next few lessons. This is my own personal grieving over the fact that (a) there were many heavy pressures on us spawned by that explosive growth, and (b) our responses to some of those pressures moved us ever closer to adopting the attitudes, attributes, and values of the for-profit world. But I believe that if you're going to share leadership of a nonprofit agency today, you must know how it got to where it is from where it was, just so that you can understand and manage the ever-continuing dynamics of the pressures and responses that are not only still following us, but that promise to increase in intensity.

Just get a 1901 street-scene photograph from any city of your choice. Then compare it with the same scene today. The latter may have a higher resolution (I don't know what that term means, but you probably do), but the more recent one will also show a higher level of action, intensity, confusion, and even chaos. And so it is with the nonprofit world from that one date to the other. The aspect to which I referred above is, I repeat, simply *growth*—the explosive growth in the number of nonprofit agencies in our world. This occurred especially in the last 35 years of the 1900s, during which there was a 100 percent increase in the number of agencies, from approximately 700,000 to approximately 1,400,000. That's what made it a tough time. That then induced the profound change (competition for survival, you'll remember) that in turn spawned a lot of influences on us and responses by us. Those influences and responses are what we shall explore. But first, and for later comparison, let's do another Lewis scenario.

The first part of the 20th century was a relatively quiet time for you and me. (We're back in our respective roles again. This time we're a small, liberal arts college: You're the president and I'm the board.) My role in the governance of the agency was limited and precise, which made it easy for you. I had no elaborate job description. It was just implicit that with respect to the college, I would be expected to (a) declare or affirm its mission, (b) select you to manage the place, (c) see to the furnishing of the resources, and then (d) stay the hell out of the way. This last, I must emphasize, was a full and equivalent part of the protocol between us. You'd (a) take it from there; (b) call me to an occasional board meeting; (c) tell me in polite but unilateral fashion what you'd been doing and expected to do in the future; (d) trot out your senior staff to review the highlights of the football season and take up enough meeting time to make me think it was worthwhile my traveling there; (e) entertain me at dinner, at which the college glee club would perform; and (f) send me off smiling and content. There might be one or two board committees reporting—probably just the nominating committee and almost always some sort of financial committee to keep us on our toes about the money needs of the institution. This latter committee had an honest name—it was not yet euphemized into a development committee. I served until I died, resigned, or became incontinent. As I looked around at the "me's" in the board room, we all looked quite alike (white), and we enjoyed the fact that we thought alike on almost everything, including politics.

And both you and I enjoyed a position of almost unquestioned respect in our communities—I call it the "halo effect." It was endowed quite naturally on the leaders of almost all nonprofit agencies and institutions at that time. We could do virtually no wrong, and the listing in my obituary of my service on two or more nonprofit boards absolutely assured me of a high-blown eulogy at my funeral. No one questioned the institution's right to exist, or even the quality of its functioning.

By the 1970s, the explosive growth had come to our world like a plague. The factors that it spawned were staggering in their number, importance, and effect on our lives in this once-calm world. As we identify and explore them, you'll notice (a) how they interrelate—no one of them is isolated from any of the others; and (b) that each one of them brings us closer to the attributes of the for-profit world. We start to behave ourselves just as if we were the for-profits. This behavior creates a challenge that goes beyond taking the necessary steps to survive. And those steps could well direct us away from what should be the soul and spirit of the nonprofit world. Just watch how all these things close in on us.

LESSON 25—COMPETITION FOR SURVIVAL

We're in It

Let's look at higher education for purposes of this lesson, because it's a good example. As more and more of us flooded the higher educational institutions—and this really began with the advent of the G.I. bill toward the end of World War II—changes came rapidly for us in the nonprofit educational field. This legislation marked a turning point in post-high school education. The community college, a relatively new concept based on the old junior college model (but now with public funding) was rediscovered and encouraged, and more than 3,000 of them sprang up. This helped to meet the demand for classroom space and instruction, but also helped to crowd the field of institutions offering services. These new colleges created not only new educational programs, but also a huge new clamor for sharing the educational dollar, irrespective of its source (i.e., student fees, public funding, or individual and institutional grants). Some of the state-supported senior colleges and universities were the first to feel the squeeze. After all, they had to share the educational budget of their state with these upstart new institutions. Some, quite belatedly, tried to head off the problem by creating branch campuses serving geographical areas that were previously of little interest to them. Clearly, there was competition for *monetary* survival.

But the competition for funding between these two types of institutions had its own additional, related element of competition—enrollment. And because the state subsidy was determined in part by enrollment, the pressure to recruit and retain student head count became a preoccupation and a contest.

Then, the private, independent colleges and universities also got into the competition game, at least with respect to the funding part. In the earlier days before this growth change, state-supported institutions and private institutions had a sort of detente. The "publics," enjoying public financial support, stayed away from foundation support, leaving that to the "privates." But that polite arrangement was despoiled as the publics' competition with *each other* began to reach frantic proportions. And in that frantic state, they began to look to private and foundation support as well. Soon, the privates were getting into the *public* treasury, both by way of loan and grant programs for students in the privates themselves as well as by an expansion of research grants to those privates doing advance studies in the pure and social sciences.

So now what? Well, I'd like to give you some comfort about this, but the fact is that the trend continues. And the most important point to be made here is that competition for survival applies not only to education, but to every one of us in the whole field of nonprofits—health care, cultural arts, community service in its many manifestations, and religion in *its* many manifestations. So, ED, whatever field you're in, gird your loins and, as ED, insist that I gird mine for the rest of the challenge. If people ask you what that means, just tell them that "gird" (put a girdle on) was used in *Beowulf,* and that "loins" refers to some part of the body between the ribs and the hip bones. Each of the agencies will now struggle to survive: Agencies will not any longer just keep on surviving because they're a non-profit agency. It'll now be a struggle for all of us. Just watch what we do.

Diversion: One more thought before we go on—the word "chaos." It comes over to us unchanged from its origin in ancient Greek. It looks different in Greek, of course, because their letters were in different form, but it sounds the same in Greek and English. Its meaning in ancient times portends perfectly with what we have here in the new environment for nonprofits. It meant "a state in which everything gets in the way of everything else."

LESSON 26—NOW YOU'RE INTO MARKETING AND PROGRAM DELIVERY

Another Sign of the New Era

Take, for example, recruitment in the higher education field. Before the post-World War II changes and the chaos that I described above invaded the field, the colleges and universities went their quiet, dignified ways catering to their usual enrollees, who were later called "traditional students" in order to distinguish them from the upstarts now daring to go beyond high school. The term traditional students referred to those of us who went through high school or prep school with the specific, declared aim of continuing at the college level, more specifically, the senior college level. If you were affiliated with a senior-college-type institution, you carefully selected your incoming freshmen from an oversubscribed list of applicants. Those who were admitted were then handed a catalog of courses and the dates and times when they would meet. Usually, this meant mornings and early afternoons, and mostly on weekdays. This was just perfect for the traditional student and quite accommodating to the preferences of faculty and staff. Take it or leave it.

The only semblance of competition during those days came in the form of competition among the applicants to gain *admission* to the institutions of their choice. Then bam! We had returning veterans of World War II buoyed by financial support for more education from the G.I. bill— some with families and jobs. They were a tempting "market." Then, at the same time, we had a surge of women (imagine!) seeking equal educational opportunities as those for men. A fad called lifelong education entered both our vocabulary and our consciousness, and "seniors" decided that they wanted to go back to classes. Then there were the undertrained thousands who sought better positions in the growing technological fields.

I'm not an educational historian, but I saw enough to understand that the higher education institutions recognized the possibilities. What a solution for them, if only they could accommodate these forces! If only they could change their ways. If only they could do some, yes, *marketing*. If only they could adapt to some new methods of *program delivery*. Well, it didn't take long. "Marketing" became so important that even the stodgiest of institutions engaged a director of marketing, and the board itself created a marketing committee, recognizing the importance of the concept. Accommodation to the non-traditional students? Not a problem. Come to us. Classes and courses on days, evenings, weekends, when and as you need them. Courses over the Internet. Courses and classes at seven of our local high schools. Just tell us what your plans are. We can help.

You see, we've now joined in the direct competition phase of operations through the mechanisms of marketing and program delivery. The other colleges in the area are no longer our *colleagues* in education; they're our *competitors,* and we feel that we have to outdo them in enrollment somehow if we want to survive. I guess you have to conclude that we in the nonprofit world may not yet be at the cutthroat stage, but clearly we aren't nearly as nice as we used to be.

LESSON 27—HONE UP ON YOUR PUBLIC RELATIONS

Another Sign of the Times

This will be a short one because I have no patience for it; it makes me crabby.

"And it shall follow as the night the day" that if you're into marketing and a more accommodating program delivery (as the previous lesson specifies), you've got to get into the art and science of public relations, known to the smugly all-knowing as PR. You realize, of course, that the quoted part of the previous sentence is pure Shakespeare. The rest of it is pure trash. It's dumped on us as we move inexorably, but sadly, toward taking on the commercial attributes of the for-profit world, the natural consequences of growth and competition.

I should not be surprised if, in the highly competitive arena of hospital care, we shall soon see an advertisement or two extolling its valet parking facilities, its Sealey mattresses, its percale towels, its elaborate menus, or the cheery curtains on its windows or the television sets and extension phones and hair dryers in the patients' bathrooms. "Remember, have your next heart attack with us. Send for our new brochure. No obligation. We'll keep the light on for you." And in our first meeting with our newly engaged PR firm, the first question put to us has to do *not* with our hospital's morbidity rate or our college's graduation rate, but with whether or not we have a logo. Or the firm may recommend that we become part of some "cause-related" advertising with some for-profit enterprise. For example, our animal humane society can agree that the local furrier may use our name in his advertisements if he gives five percent of his Christmas season sales to our agency. This *kind* of arrangement is made quite frequently. In my impatient brain, this is regarded as, at best, sleeping with the enemy; at worst, treason. Increasingly, however, it's regarded by our PR advisors, euphemistically, as "cause-related" PR.

I hope that you, as ED, can deal with that foolishness better than I can.

LESSON 28—CONSUMERISM

It's Part of the Mix

This lesson is part of the mix that we've already covered in Lessons 24 through 27. In preparing to write this lesson, I looked in my *Webster's Third New International Dictionary* for a definition of "consumerism."[1] At first, I was surprised that it wasn't there. But then, I realized that the concept had not yet taken hold in the consciousness of humankind at the time of the printing. However, I did find an entry—it was "consumer sovereignty"—and it fit exactly into the essence of this lesson. It was defined as "the economic power exercised by the preferences of consumers in a free market."

It reminded me immediately of the actions of many of our nonprofits to accommodate to these "preferences" and thus to respond to "economic power." Some of these accommodations resulted in true benefits to the society and

---

[1] *Webster's Third New International Dictionary, Unabridged.* (New York: G & C Merriam Company, 1971).

the community and are to be commended. I refer, for example, to the "traditional student" syndrome. Before the sensitivity to consumerism (I'll use the word anyway, because you know what I mean), most colleges other than those that were "open-door" institutions sought their new students among high school graduates who showed a certain level of academic achievement. As economic power became more of a consideration, however, compromises became the rule. The need to attain desired enrollment levels influenced colleges to go more deeply into their candidate pools. If there were some academic deficiency, they offered "remedial" courses right there on campus to bring the particular student up to speed, to where he/she should have been in the "traditional" mode. That became an actual part of the curriculum, and those courses took on their own category/name: "remedial." And soon after, in a show of extreme sensitivity, those courses became known as "developmental" rather than "remedial." I hope you agree with me that this was a positive change. Other examples of good change include—again, in my view—the tendency of single-sex colleges to become coeducational.

But then again, because everyone involved is a mere human, some of the changes they hit on seem a bit mindless. They usually start with the question of popular opinion—preferences of consumers without necessary regard to anything else. For me, coed dormitories come first to mind.

On a recent visit to the state-run universities in the Republic of China, I met with one of the university presidents in a city south of Taipei. He was particularly interested in the trend in our country to allow coed dorms. He asked me about the rationale, and I gave him the usual party line—realities of life and all that sort of stuff. I remember well his response: "In the university system of our Republic, we have very limited accommodations, so only those students who show the highest intellectual promise are admitted. They represent the young people, men and women, whom we consider worthy of the state's investment in their future and the future of Taiwan. If these, our best and our brightest young men and women, cannot contrive some way to get together without living together in a dormitory, we have probably selected the wrong young people." Considering the old adage that "lust laughs at locksmiths," I think he was right on target.

And there's another interesting aspect of consumerism—the new terminology used by some of our nonprofit agencies. I was startled recently when, at the community college where I have an academic appointment, I first heard an administrator refer to our students as "customers." I understand that this term is now in common use with respect to the people who receive our services, not only in the educational field, but also in the health care field, and probably many other fields that I have not yet heard about. "Students," "patients," and like terms are out of favor, and "customers" is the term on the ascendancy. This troubles me. Along with the term comes an inarguable adage: The customer is always right. This is patently the case in the for-profit world, but should it apply to us? Well, it already has.

Take the university as the traditional center of learning, the institution that by its own mission statement fosters learning at the undergraduate and graduate levels in the arts, the sciences, the humanities, and the professions. As increasing attention is paid to "the economic power exercised by the preferences of consumers" (remember that phrase?), certain things begin to happen to that university. There is underenrollment in its School of Architecture, and that school soon closes because it cannot "support" itself on student fees. (Is it the victim of the university's sudden discovery of that "bottom-line" thing?) Then there is underenrollment in its Department of Classical Studies, and that is soon abandoned because it cannot support itself on student fees. The same fate is suffered by the university press and the Department of Medieval English, and the courses in French Impressionism and a few other of the more exotic fields of study. So, that specter of economic power—the attitude that students are customers and that the customer is always right—soon makes us ask the question of whether or not our university, as it abandons its overall goals to the popularity contest, is still a university.

LESSON 29—DIVERSITY

Important but Complex

If you go back to the pre-1970s board meeting scene that I described in Lesson 24, you'll note that I described myself and my colleague trustees at that meeting as lookalikes. Well, we certainly were. We were all white and all from roughly the same economic, social, educational, and cultural strata. Not a sign of a woman or a person of color. Diversity? The very term was frightening. After all, we were getting along so well together. Diversity meant differences in attitudes, perspectives, and points of view, and those differences meant the kind of change that would likely be antithetical to (if not outrightly destructive of) the gentle pace of our discussions at the board table. Our uneasiness came from the fact that at the time, we really didn't appreciate what the soul of trusteeship was all about. We really didn't appreciate that we were vested with a public interest and charged with a public trust, and that the overall public perspective had to be included in our deliberations. Our student body (and, ultimately, our alumni) was becoming more diverse and increasingly skeptical of governance by the "old boy" standards. We, on the other hand, were somewhat slowly becoming aware that society was on the brink of enormous social upheaval and that maybe—yes, just maybe—we had to broaden our horizons. As there began to emerge the massive social changes that were just over that last hill, there was the implicit demand that we change our board structure so that we were much more capable of handling one of the areas of accountability of a board—to interpret society to the institution, and to interpret the institution to society. This simply meant that the face of the board should more closely reflect the face of society, and particularly the face of that segment of society or of the community that the agency was purporting to serve.

And so diversity took hold. It may have disturbed the quiescence of a lot of us old boys, but it certainly made for a more sensitive and responsive, and a less paternalistic and patronizing, leadership mechanism. Fewer of our decisions at the board table were unanimous, and many of them were compromises, but in my opinion, in the long run, leadership underwent a healthy transition. Diversity has now become so engrained in the values of the nonprofit world that funding sources and accreditation agencies demand that it be one of the characteristics of the leadership team.

LESSON 30—STAKEHOLDERS

Who's Driving the Bus?

There's a third possible title for this lesson: "The Sea of Conflicting Expectations." Just remember some of the stuff in our lessons on program delivery (Lesson 26), consumerism (Lesson 28), and diversity (Lesson 29). Well, this ties right in.

You'll note that previously, I personally objected to calling the students of our colleges or the patients of our hospitals "customers." I feel the same regarding the recipients of our social services at our homes for runaway girls, or the congregants of our places of worship, as for both of whom the term customers seems ridiculous. I should hope that both they and we feel that our level of human (and humane) concern for each other as part of the nonprofit world transcends that of the marketplace. Yet, whereas once we held out our services to them on a take-it-or-leave-it basis (remember the traditional college catalog and its unilateral offerings with no necessary accommodation to the course registrant?), we later realized that although they are not customers, they are categories of people who nonetheless have a "stake" in our functioning. We further reasoned that the "stakehold" interest could (and should) well influence us to think beyond our previous inflexibility.

It was an easy next step to realizing that the stakeholders of our college were not just our governance and management leadership, not just our faculty and students, but also our alumni, parents of students, institutional funders, donors, accreditation agencies, graduate schools to which we sent our own graduates, municipalities in which we established our campuses, residential and business communities adjacent to and surrounding our campuses, the Internal Revenue Service, and heaven knows who else. And because every decision at the board table could have *some kind* of a direct or ripple effect on each one of those stakeholders, we had to be mindful of that fact and maneuver our way through the minefield of conflicting expectations.

The answer to the question of who's driving the bus isn't quite easy—it's somewhere between the two of us, you and me, the ED and the board. But the maneuvering is a few times more difficult than it once was. But if we're a really good leadership team, we'll make the tough decisions—no matter how tough they are—when we must. But it will not be without first identifying the laundry list of potentially affected stakeholders and whether and to what extent their respective and collective stakes should be weighed in the balance. Your board is going to rely on you to assure it that the resolution before us for a vote has your assurance that everything on the laundry list has been given your professional consideration. The answer to the question of this lesson, "Who's Driving the Bus?" is simple. It's you. I'll tell you where we want to go; you'll take the route to get us there.

LESSON 31—ASSESSMENT

The Lifting of the Halos

Several lessons back (Lesson 24, to be exact), we referred to the halos that we in the nonprofit world were almost automatically rewarded. We were in a field of effort that exuded propriety, altruism, honesty, integrity, almost nobility.

Diversion: Those words remind me of something. When we traveled with the Marx Brothers, Groucho had a comment on everything. In one of his movies, he played the role of a college president speaking before his board of trustees. He stated, with appropriate pomposity, that to be a good trustee, one must show honesty, integrity, generosity, and altruism. That sounds just right, doesn't it—even coming from Groucho Marx? But I must forewarn you, he wasn't finished. For then, with a facial expression that was somewhat between a grin and a leer, he said, "If you can fake all of that, you've got it made!"

But unfortunately, we can't discount Groucho's frivolity too quickly. Because too many of our trustees did too much faking, and soon we came under the pall of skepticism, cynicism, and doubt as to the extent to which our reputation for perfection and saintly qualities was really deserved. The scandals of the 1990s—National United Way, Covenant House, The National Association of American Colored Persons, and Adelphi University (to name just a few)—all took away our sacred status. Further, as the effects of the survival competition took hold and we were acting more and more like the for-profits, society began to wonder if we were really fulfilling our public trust. This then led to the question of *how well*, and this led quite naturally to the request of *show us*. So, assessment, here we are. And you, my dear ED, are over your head in it.

The basic tenet with respect to assessment is this: The board of trustees has been charged with the overall monitoring authority of the agency (in one respect, that's what governance is), and that means seeing to it that in this competitive environment, all phases of its operations are in the "commendable" class. And you (yes, you again) must see to it that the board realizes this as part of its existence.

LESSON 32—ASSESSMENT, ITS MANY MANIFESTATIONS

Our Potential Preoccupation

The concept of assessment in the nonprofit world has many meanings and many faces. Initially, there is the *needs* assessment. This usually applies to the study to be made for the purpose of determining if there is the desirability for a particular proposed new agency. We're not going to deal with that because we're assuming that you're up and running—that the need has already been determined. So we turn to the more applicable aspects of assessment, now that we already exist and function, namely, (a) assessment of your (the ED's) performance, (b) assessment of my (the board's) performance, and (c) program assessment. The word "assess" in its verb form has many meanings. For our purposes, I select these two: *to analyze critically/to adjudge merit*. By going through the assessment process, then, we are really trying to determine our agency's worthiness to exist and solicit support. What a strange and remarkable shift from the past! Going back to that benign board meeting in Lesson 24, there wasn't the slightest hint of inquiry on the part of anyone there that worthiness was even an issue. And so it was with almost every nonprofit agency of those times. "I exist, therefore I exist." Or, better still, "I have existed, therefore I deserve to continue to exist." But no longer, and *you* must make your board and your agency understand that. Because as you know from the last few lessons, competition for survival (and, of course, for support as well) brought some new standards that had to be achieved before those halos were to be handed out again. Worthiness was no longer to be assumed—it had to be proved by fairly strong evidence. So, let's do some assessments, Okay? Sure, let's do some. But how?

The "how" then became something somewhere among science, art, and mystery—but with a little more PR thrown in. And some aspects of our functioning were more easily susceptible to critical analysis, more easily adjudged as to merit. Perhaps the easiest of the three with which we're dealing is that that pertains to you, the ED.

Assessment of the ED's Performance

Exhibit 1–1, specifying the areas of a board's accountability when acting *as a board*, lists one among those that relate to the board's colleague in leadership, its ED: you. It's an area of accountability that we call "non-delegable," because it's such an important part of our professional/personal relationship that the board alone must undertake the process. It's likely to be the easiest of the three because it's likely that there is sufficient documentation to guide us. Any fair system of assessment of the ED requires that there be (a) agreement as to the list of expectations pertaining to the ED's performance, (b) a mechanism to ensure that these expectations are clearly known to the ED, (c) a reasonable period of time during which the measurement of that performance can take place, and (d) a fair system of open and *mutual* communication (we'll get to that *mutual* part in a moment) about how it is to be done. The documentation to which I refer could be any and all of the "things" that usually articulate, expressly or by implication, what the agency expects of her. These could include

- the agency's bylaws describing the ED's responsibilities, if provided therein

- the ED's employment agreement, assuming there is one

- the goals and objectives for the agency as set forth in its plan

- the agency policies adopted by the board and requiring articulation by the ED

- the ED's own written statement of her goals for the period in question

But here, by way of repetition and emphasis, are the big provisos: The ED must understand these to have been the board's areas of expectation, and the ED must have had sufficient time during which to show her leadership skills in meeting those expectations.

Important Digression: In Exhibit 1–1, we come upon another of the board's non-delegable areas of accountability, that is, its role in "supporting, advising, and encouraging the ED." Here's where that becomes pertinent. It's another of those annoying "Lewis rules," and it goes like this: There's no such thing as the unilateral assessment of the ED's performance. It should be assessed only against the backdrop of how well the board itself performs its own areas of accountability, especially this one. Thus, in the *communication* phase of the ED's assessment process, she must be given the opportunity to visit this issue of how well the board itself has performed, and the board people involved in the process should invite such a discussion.

Assessment of the Board's Performance

This is a relatively new concept, but you, as ED, must see to it that it becomes part of your organizational culture. I don't know exactly how you're going to bring it about— maybe by just forcefully "advising" your chair that it must be done on occasion. For too many years, it was considered taboo—an actual insult to these generous, altruistic souls who, after all, were just well-meaning "volunteers." Well, I hope we've straightened out the world on that issue in Lesson 3. But it took more than some Lewis ravings in front of a class to make the change toward making the board show *its* worthiness. It all goes back to competition and the struggle for survival and, as part of that, the requirement that, compared to other boards looking for support for their agencies, the board be a "good" board and know its real role in the life of the agency. There was a convergence of influences on this matter. First, the funding sources demanded evidence of a high level of board accountability, and that meant requiring a board to know what it should and should not be doing. Occasionally, this demand came in the form of a suggestion that the board conduct a retreat at which it could devote time to a self-study or an equivalent event with a consultant or the like—an occasion during which it could get away from the issues that usually dominate its meeting agendas and just muse about itself and its perceived areas of strength and concern. I have conducted scores of those events, some of them fun, some not. I'll tell you about them later (Lesson 39). Second, the accreditation agencies joined the trend.

Another Diversion: Surprisingly, until relatively recently, in their evaluation of the agency's worthiness of accreditation or re-accreditation—a college or a hospital or a social service agency—the accreditation group seldom paid attention to the board of trustees. They looked at all phases of programs and staff matters and the executive officers, but boards were pretty much off limits. You know the situation: It was just more of that "after-all-they're-just-volunteers" rubbish. What's more, in most instances, the board didn't even know that the accreditation process was going on (*you,* you rascal of an ED, never even told us!), and they may not have wished to be part of the process anyway. This is unfortunate, because if the board is involved in the process, it then has the most wonderful opportunity to learn firsthand more about its agency than it might in any other way. It can then have a better objective and realistic view of "worthiness" than it would otherwise get. There is no better basis for then making the policy decisions that can control the agency's future.

Some years ago, I had the occasion to serve on a visiting team of a college accreditation agency. We were sent to the campus of a prestigious small college for our site visit as the last part of preparing our recommendation as to re-accreditation. The college had already done the laborious and minutely detailed introspective self-study required by the process, and we on the team had studied it carefully. It was unusual in one significant way. Although it had the usual entries stipulating the college's self-perceived "areas of strength and areas of concern," in this case, the areas of concern were listed right up there in the opening pages of the text, not way, way back. Several of those areas of concern, I noticed, involved governance-level matters that would be within the province of the board for future action and improvement. (Peculiarly, the areas of "concern" about the board had apparently been "uncovered" not by the board itself, but by other college elements.) We then went about the campus inspecting, interviewing, and perusing records and dormitories and athletic fields and library stacks. We met with scores of college constituencies—faculty, students, administration, and staff in every support field. When I received our agenda for these meetings, prior to making the actual site visit, I noticed that it did not include any trustees, and I mentioned this to our team chair. She, in turn, mentioned it to the president of the college, who then arranged to invite our team to a hastily convened dinner with "a few of our trustees who live nearby."

After dinner, our team chair invited comments from team members—a kind of courtesy report to the trustees as to why we were there. When it was my turn, I complimented the board on the healthy state of the college (as did all other team members), but then addressed the self-study. I spoke with admiration of the fact that the self-study was so "up front"—literally so—in setting forth its areas of concern (most self-studies hide that section somewhere toward the end), and that I assumed that that would make it easy for the board to seize quickly on the issues that required governance-level attention. As I did so, I noticed two different emerging facial expressions around the table: The president looked uneasy as I spoke, and the trustees looked puzzled. It soon became clear that the trustees didn't have the slightest idea what I was talking about. They were, until that moment, unaware of the details of the re-accreditation process, and only dimly aware that their college was going through it, and they drew blanks when I referred to the self-study. Later on, when our team met to rehearse its report to our accreditation agency, I suggested that we report the board's non-involvement in this important process as a deficiency. My teammates, however, all holding high positions in *administration* in their home institutions, many of them as EDs, saw nothing amiss in the situation. It was another manifestation of the "you-trustees-are-just-volunteers" mindset. They could not equate trusteeship with ownership of the college, and expressed the idea that assessing the board's performance was a mere frivolity. I hope that when you're dealing with governance assessment, you won't take that attitude about your board or, more important, allow your board to take that attitude about itself. Now back to the new influences on trustee assessment.

I noted above that joining the foundations were (surprise, surprise!) the accreditation agencies themselves. In response to this new trend, and, in fact, joining as another of the influences, two prestigious organizations involved in board development devised some rather brilliant self-study questionnaires to be used by boards on such occasions. Both are headquartered in Washington, DC: The Association of Governing Boards of Universities and Colleges, which concentrates on boards of higher education agencies, and the National Center for Nonprofit Boards, which accommodates most other nonprofit agency boards. Look them up in the telephone directory and buy their forms relating to trustee assessment when the spirit moves you. Then go to your board chair and convince him that it's time for action. Even trustees themselves are beginning to get the spirit. But it'll take *your* nudging.

Program Assessment

This is the most complex of the three aspects of assessment devolving on you and the board because it gets mixed up with the issues covered in Lesson 23, the myth about the clear distinction between governance and management. I have repeatedly declared that the board should be involved in the agency's mission-related and goal-related issues, leaving the program-related issues to you. But I've also noted that that protocol exists only as an internal working formula between board and staff, and is not binding outside of the agency. Society, the community, and our various stakeholders hold the *board* accountable for responding (or seeing to it that *you* respond) commendably to all three levels of issue—mission, goals, *and programs*. So don't get your nose out of joint when I, the board, get into the act of program assessment. Yet here again, I stumble on the big *however*. However, *how* do I, the board, do it? I'm not a professional, as you are, in the field in which the agency operates. I'm not an educator or a health care specialist or a social worker or a graphic or performing artist or a clergyman. Oh sure, common sense gives me some guidelines. If our hospital has a 100 percent morbidity rate, or if our college has a 0 percent graduation rate, or if our stage performances or symphony concerts draw pitifully few subscribers and many horrifying reviews—well, you get the picture. Although any one of those instances is devastating to the agency, it sure makes it easy for the board to draw its conclusion about the worthiness of the programs. But where does the board go in a less well-defined situation? The answer is easy: *It looks to you to furnish the information and the criteria on which that is based!*

So although the board has the accountability for assessing program quality, the method for assuring the board as to the level of quality is back on your shoulders. I, as the board, can of course tell if the orchestra is consistently out of tune or if the lead actor is consistently forgetting his lines. But by my sitting in on a class in economics, I can't tell if the educational program is going well. And by my standing there in the operating room and watching brain surgery, I have no way of knowing the level of the surgeon's skill. I do *my* part by demanding of *you* the assurance that I need as to program quality so that I, in turn, get the sense that I've fulfilled my accountability.

That still leaves open the question of how *you* do it. Here are a few of the models.

1.   Survey the "consumers" of the agency's services by interviews or questionnaire.

2.   Survey the program staff by interviews or questionnaire.

3.   Use the quantitative approach; namely, count how *many* people we serve. This may be a valid way of determining the relative worthiness of two agencies in the same field of activity, but not always even then, because the criterion may be im-

possible to determine. For example, if the question in the mind of the donor is which of two churches should be funded, it has been suggested that the determination should be made on the basis of how many souls have been saved from perdition per hour of preaching. That can be determined, I imagine, only after the fact and by maintaining an actual count at the Pearly Gates. But this quantitative approach can be completely inappropriate in determining relative worthiness as between agencies in different fields. As an example of this, take the American Red Cross. On the "numbers" issue, it would probably win hands down against almost any other agency. It is consistently coming to the aid of thousands of us every time there's a flood or an earthquake or some other uncontrollable natural disaster. Where would we be without it? But where would the quantitative approach leave the tiny Irish Music Academy (that is not its real name) with whose board I once did some consulting? It has nine trustees, two teachers, and about fifteen students, and has as its mission the preservation of the literature and culture of the tin whistle and the hammered dulcimer. How worthy is *it?* I personally, as a musician and a sentimentalist, think it is very worthy. For without that brave band of eccentrics, the literature and culture of the tin whistle and the hammered dulcimer might soon become extinct.

4. Use the common sense approach. By this, I mean having us all realize that the worthiness of a nonprofit agency—justification for its existence, financial support, acceptance by the community, and continued favorable tax treatment—is more subjective than anything else. We in this wondrous nonprofit world have no bottom line, no

simple way of determining "success." Numbers are virtually meaningless because trying to determine how many (or few) people we educate or cure or advise or help along with life doesn't account for how many others related to them are touched by way of the ripple effect. (I recall one woman, a former Girl Scout, telling me—now 20 years later—that her family was still benefiting from what she learned as a member of that organization so long ago.) We have senses, we have instincts, and we can observe. We shouldn't be expecting efficiency or slick mechanisms to tell us how worthy we are.

I'd like to go back to Lesson 9 and to Emperor Asoka. I repeat here my suggestion in that lesson: Let's just get our board and staff together and ask the three questions: (a) Are we rendering humane, compassionate, and benevolent service to the community? (b) Are we monitored by people of honesty and truthfulness? (c) Are we administered by a competent executive and staff? I strongly believe that we're all people of sufficient good faith and goodwill to be able to discuss all aspects of all three questions. And I believe further that a record of the discussions will give us as accurate an answer to the question of worthiness as any other method we could devise.

All of this is more of an art and an instinct than it is a science. Shall we ever be successful in selling that idea?

CHAPTER 7

Working with Other Nonprofits

T his could be a sound strategy or an unfortunate fad. Approach it carefully. If we use the term "strategic alliance" we are emphasizing our copy-cat tendency--emulating the for-profit world with its fashioanble mergers and growth for growth's sake without regard to issues of soul. That's what I call an ufortunate fad. If, on the other hand, we seek a cooperative arrangement with a sister nonprofit agency with our primary aim being improved service to the community, that's what I call a sound strategy. This chapter states the case.

LESSON 33—STRATEGIC ALLIANCES

Just a Fancy Term, or More? Or, We Can Argue Either Way

Let's get this much straight: The trend toward creating strategic alliances among nonprofits is growing and flourishing. Some alliances work well; some are abysmal failures. I'm going to devote three whole lessons to the concept. This one will be somewhat of a general discussion. The next, Lesson 34, will deal with the ideal circumstances for approaching a strategic alliance—in our case, a merger project—successfully. Then, in Lesson 35, we'll see the unexpected and sometimes insidious influences that negate even those "ideal circumstances." You're going to need all of this as we enter this new era for nonprofits where we imitate, each day increasingly, the for-profit world. Here goes.

The nonprofit world has been assailed by scores of new expressions and new concepts, as you've seen from a lot of what we had to say in the last several lessons. I'm reminded of the 1960s and 1970s, when the social workers grabbed hold of our language and added some ungrammatical psychobabble. There was "prioritize" (not a word), and "access" (a noun tortured into involuntary servitude as a verb), and "problem-solving" (for some reason considered, I guess, as a more economical way of saying "solving problems," even though it saves only one letter but requires a space for the hyphen). This last one gave some authenticity to "fundraising," which I dislike along with the others that I just mentioned. However, all of them have made their way into our ever-deteriorating language. And all of them have made their way into the vocabulary of the nonprofit world, along with some more recent gems: "interactive" (essentially meaningless) and "empowerment" (as in, permission I give to my five out-of-town daughters and sons to use my 800-line when they call me at home). For some reason, I have much less objection to "pants pressing" and "call waiting."

Digression: People have a tendency to speak before they think, and the result is frequently an aggregation of meaningless words. Whatever happened, I call out to the heavens, to the noble language of Shakespeare and Milton and Wordsworth and Churchill and Franklin D. Roosevelt and Ira Gershwin and Yip Harburg and Duke Ellington? I grieve as I experience one example after another that makes me lose hope. Like the call I received one day a few years ago when I was still in the practice of law; it was from a then-client, a woman industrialist from New York. When I answered the telephone, "Hello," she then said (inexplicably), "Are you the person with whom I am speaking?" Wouldn't you lose hope, too? But that was followed some few days later when I was changing planes at the United Airlines terminal at Chicago's O'Hare airport and going through that torture chamber of light sound in one of those hallways that required the futility of going down one escalator for the sole and obvious purpose of just going up the next. As I, along with many others, was going through that modernistic purgatory, there came over the public address system one of the most mellifluous female voices I had ever heard. She started by saying, "Attention please, attention please, this is an important announcement." We all quieted down, quite fearful, I guess, of what was next to come. And after a moment or two of tension, she came back on line and continued, "Will all O'Hare passengers who have not yet done so, please do so now." You figure it out.

The grammatical idiocy continued the next day when I was about to fly home from Seattle. I took my seat, but felt a large card under my bottom. I fished it out and studied the text in disbelief. Here is what it said: "You are seated in an exit row. This may require your assistance in the event of an emergency. This card explains your duties. If you cannot read it, please notify a flight attendant."

I rest my case. End of digression.

To make matters worse, the nonprofit world is now developing its own jargon, some examples of which we will encounter in this lesson and the next. The phrase "strategic alliances," although not grammatically incorrect, opens the possibility of changing some nonprofit habits radically but not always for the better. In its generic sense, it refers to a mechanism by which two or more nonprofit organizations create *some version of a cooperative enterprise*. It could be as simple as what the lawyers call a joint venture—two (let's use just two here) organizations team up for a limited purpose. Both deal with women's issues: One offers the services of a safe house; the other offers primary medical care services. They decide to open an office in a needy neighborhood as a referral center for women needing "first help" in either field. This is a good example of a strategic alliance for a good purpose, namely, better humane, compassionate, and benevolent service to the community (remember Asoka?). But sometimes, the concept is promoted without necessary regard for the goodness of the purpose. I refer to the economic power exercised by donors and the psychological power exercised by sloganeers.

These days, the topic of strategic alliances is popular at regional and national meetings of associations that serve the nonprofit community. And the foundations that fund nonprofits toss the term around as if it were inconsequential. My cynicism sees this as the equivalent of the sloganeers saying, "Go team up with another entity; it's the thing to do." Surely, the business world does it all the time. As for funders, it's easier to review one proposal from two newly affiliated organizations in the field of (say) domestic violence than it is to review two separate proposals. The key to whether or not it should be done, however, is the nature of the affiliation. Our example above (the joint venture) is just right. But it has become almost a mandate that the term, influenced by trends in the for-profit world, strongly suggests a merger, the legalistic mechanism whereby two (or more) agencies actually become just one—one name, one board, one ED—when previously there were two of each. Because the trend is so ensconced in our world, let's examine its aspects.

There are bad reasons for a merger as well as good reasons. The bad reasons include the fact that one of the constituent entities is suffering from a financial crisis or scandal, a programmatic crisis or scandal, or a scandal of any other type. Yet this is what most frequently motivates thoughts of a merger in the stricken agency. I forewarn you: If one of the entities looks to a merger as a means to get out of a jam, stay away! The good reasons for a merger must be built on one basic assumption—that the resultant entity will be able to serve the community in better fashion than the two entities can do separately. It should have nothing to do with "seizing a better market share" or that rot. It gets even better if both entities function well, have a strong financial footing, have good boards and good staffs, and are motivated by the aspiration of giving better service to those in need. But I must emphasize here and now that even given that ideal situation, and given the influence of funders and sloganeers, mergers in the nonprofit world are as close to anathema as one can get.

It's strange; nonprofits are so willing to take on so many attributes of the for-profits, but mergers, one of the most popular trends in the for-profit world, seem to frighten them. And it's stranger still that this should be the case among the *trustees* of the agencies to the proposed merger, who, after all, come to us mostly from the for-profit world. Strangest of all is that they tend to create pitfalls that are not really pitfalls. Watch these issues emerge in Lesson 35.

In my 46 years as a corporate lawyer, I have had a role in approximately 300 mergers in the for-profit field, but not a single one in the nonprofit field. I did not give this a thought until I joined the nonprofit world myself, and then I learned why. Discussions on the subject spoke mainly of the many pitfalls—pride of existence being one—and less of the potential benefits. How can the greater world possibly exist without our agency continuing to do the exact things that we've been doing in our exact way over the past 27 years? It can't! Pride of uniqueness, real or imagined, is another. Merge our ballet company with *theirs*? Foolishness to the extreme! Just look— our ballerinas always wear blue tutus; theirs wear yellow. Merger is unthinkable. Then there's fear of the disappearance of board-level and staff-level camaraderie. I don't know a single person on *their* board and I'm too old now to start making new friends. I'm happy with the friends I have here, and I love our ED. And furthermore, who will comprise the board of the new entity? And which one of the EDs will be *the* ED? We're a nice, comfortable organization just as we are, right? This is frequently followed by a resounding unanimous, "Right!"

But then someone, probably our most naive trustee, asks, "But a merger with them could mean serving our community better, couldn't it?" And brows become furrowed once again around the board table and the agony of introspection continues.

I was not aware of how many intricacies have to be managed in accomplishing a merger until I had my own experience with a recent one. I share with you (Lesson 35) the experience as a classic example of those intricacies. Oh yes, there were the usual and expected questions and concerns, like those set forth above. But I offer you a guide to the less obvious, sometimes manufactured issues that are likely to be encountered and just as likely to subvert the process. By using the term, "subvert," I do not mean to suggest that those who raise these issues are not well-intentioned. But as Yogi Berra was accused of saying, "It ain't over 'til it's over." And my own experience, I'm sorry to report, was such that "over" meant not ultimate success, but ultimate failure. The toe-stubbers who brought about the failure are not necessarily those who foretell failure in other merger attempts. I cite them only to make the point that you may want to expect the unexpected, the arcane, and the insidious. But first, we'll see what "went right" in my example and what should surely have foretold success.

LESSON 34—HOW TO PUT TOGETHER A NEAR-PERFECT MERGER

Eight Factors for Doing So

The scenario was perfect. In fact, if you are confronted by the possibility of a merger, I suggest that the following eight factors be used as criteria for determining the probability of success. We'll discuss later what went wrong, but the causes of the failure could never have been suspected. Meanwhile, here's the good stuff.

1. The proposed merger involved five separate 501(c) 3 agencies, each with its own facilities within the limits of a southern midwestern county. Their missions as to each other were harmonious: Each had a mission aimed at preventing, reducing, or otherwise responding to the horrors experienced by victims of domestic violence and their witnesses. One concentrated on counseling, mentoring, and referrals; two operated shelters for battered women and their children; one was essentially a neighborhood drop-in center for women with problems of any nature; and one offered legal assistance to domestic violence victims. Thus, we had sister nonprofit agencies (a) that were neighbors, (b) that were dealing with several different facets of one major social problem, (c) among which there was minimum duplication and no redundancy in service or facilities (the two that operated shelters could hardly meet the need in its entirety).

2. The idea of achieving closer consortial efforts among the agencies was conceived by the five EDs themselves. They candidly acknowledged that the sum total of their individual programs still left gaps in some kinds of service needed in the domestic violence field. They felt that by their combined, consortial efforts, by merger or otherwise, those gaps could be filled more easily. Thus, the idea of merger originated with the agencies themselves and was not thrust on them by funders or anyone else "outside."

3. The five EDs mutually acknowledged that the effort to achieve a merger required that the "project" itself (that was the term applied to the effort) have its own mission statement. In this case, it was stated to

be "better service to the community as a single entity than could be achieved by our continuing to exist and operate as five separate entities." Thus, they gave life to the project as an effort that was distinct from and in addition to their daily activities. This allowed a mindset by which they could give the project enthusiastic and energetic attention without diminution of their daily tasks.

4. Each of the five EDs acknowledged that she would not contend for any staff position in the new agency, once created. Thus, they disposed of any kind of potential for a power struggle among the professional leaders of the project.

5. Each of the five agencies was on a reasonably sound financial footing, each capable of pursuing its mission and goals and supporting its programs. Thus, the organizational health of each agency and its respective position in the community and the nonprofit world did not *require* a merger for its salvation. This constituted the best of circumstances for a merger. By contrast, it should be noted that, as stated previously, many mergers are brought to the table because one or more of the prospective parties is trying to overcome a crisis or a scandal, which is the *worst* of circumstances for a merger.

6. Based on all of the above, the plans for the project were submitted to a funding source and the planning stage itself was generously funded. Thus, the parties not only had the encouragement to go forward, but were able to do so without any call or drain on their funds for regular programmatic activities.

7. The project engaged a consultant (me) to monitor the project and, at my suggestion, engaged an independent auditor and an independent lawyer to pur-

sue the "due diligence" part of the procedure. This was necessary so that each party would be assured of the financial and legalistic status and integrity of the others. In this connection, each ED pledged full and open discussion of all aspects of her agency excepting, of course, client confidentiality.

8.   The planning phase was carefully scripted and included, among a host of other steps and activities:

- Periodic but frequent meetings of the EDs in order to exchange information about their respective agencies (i.e., programs, funding sources, staffing, governance structure, perceived gaps in service) and identify issues emerging from that information that required resolution before the merger could be concluded.

- The creation of a project-wide "work group," consisting of the ED and her designee (usually a trustee) from each agency. (This group would also meet frequently and make recommendations as to how any such emerging issues should be resolved. The group was also responsible for keeping all personnel within their respective agencies aware of all that was going on in the project.)

- A program of interviewing representatives of the stakeholders in the domestic violence field (e.g., funders, government agencies, law enforcement agencies, mental health experts, physicians, victims and their families, other social service agencies) in order to add to the information for improving service to the community.

- Culmination of the results of all of the above in the creation of a "document for decision" specifying the steps to be taken (i.e., legalistic, administrative, and programmatic) in order to effect the merger.

Sounds good, doesn't it? It sure does. In other words, as to *this* proposed merger, the environment surrounding the project was ideal and the process was carefully thought out and, we thought, enthusiastically supported. It couldn't fail. If you provide for the same set of factors in *your* proposed merger, all will go well. See you in the next lesson.

LESSON 35—NOT SO FAST, MY FRIENDS

Some Classic Toe-Stubbers

I am reminded of Shakespeare's "dram of e'il" [evil], referred to in *Hamlet*. This particular e'il is not an elision of the word "evil" in its usual sense of meaning as bad or insidious intent. It really refers to the unexpected fault or weakness in one's makeup that can bring down a prince, or his princedom, or his fortune in life, or even his plan. This was the theme of so many of the Greek tragedies of Sophocles and Euripides. Here in our merger example, there were several such drams. Each evolved into the category of toe-stubbers that frustrated the eventual full achievement of the process. And each was based on false pride or paranoia or misinformation or groundless fear or an attack of illogic.

1. After we were well into the project, we became bogged down in a sudden attack of lack of agreement over definitions. It was then that I began to realize that hurdles were going to be thrown into the path of progress. The first involved an unexpected controversy over the term "domestic violence." There was no dispute over the "violence" part, but the "domestic" part caused enough trouble to create doubt in the minds of some few as to the exact meaning of that word as used in the project's mission statement. Did it pertain only to spousal disruptions? Or to violence among non-spouses or other couples in the home setting? Or between par-

ents and children? Or between siblings? This lack of agreement gradually turned into *disagreement,* the intensity of which began to permeate the other activities of the project. What started as a polite, almost intellectual debate on word meanings that had previously been assumed, turned acrimonious. Were the differences really that important? The answer to that question is simple—probably not, because the experiences of the five constituent agencies over the past several years had already given clear meaning to the term. Nonetheless, the dram of e'il began its insidious infection. It was starting to take the form of distrust, pride of existence, and fear of change. The definition controversy was just the excuse for foot-dragging. There's more.

2. Each agency considered itself a "feminist" organization. The staff of each agency was all female and the members of their boards of trustees were, in the majority, women. But there was that kind of a big *however,* however, that we've seen so frequently in this manuscript. There was a disparity in their respective definitions (again) of "feminist"—a disparity that may surprise you as it did me. No, it had nothing necessarily to do with the difference in intensity of their feelings as to what most of us think of as feminist issues: like unfair treatment of women by men or by society, or unequal treatment in business or the professions, or failure of the passage of the Equal Rights Amendment, as examples; or even the exploitation of women as sex objects in advertising or the entertainment media. It had nothing to do with willingness to storm the barricades or march in parades supporting women's issues. Not at all. *It had to do with the form of the governance and management mode of the agency.* Here's what I encountered. One of the agencies defined itself as the only *real* feminist organization of the five; in fact, the word "orga-

nization" offended it. It defined the "feminist agency" as one that *had no hierarchical management structure*. That, I and the other agencies were told, was *the* criterion for being a "feminist" agency. In that agency, we were told, the concept of an ED did not exist and hold title, and all agency-wide decisions were to be reached by agency-wide consensus. No one was to give orders to anyone else. Consensual decisions would determine what was to be done in any given situation.

When I heard all of that, I began to believe that I had joined an Alice in Wonderland tea party, and for good reason. First, I had actually met that agency's ED, who introduced herself to me as such. Second, I had met two of its trustees (one being the board chair), and each stated that it was the first they heard of *that*. But more to the point, and inexplicably, their representatives on the work group took the position that it sounded like a good idea anyway, and that the other agencies would have to agree that this would be the mode of operation for the merged enterprise. Not only was this startlingly idiotic, but it came too late in the process for even superficial consideration by the others. The feminist agency therefore dropped out. I cite this not to try to adjudicate the term "feminist," but only as an example of how unexpected, ephemeral, and ghostlike issues must be listed as a risk factor in any merger process. Here again, I can conclude only that the lack of agreement on definitions was a manufactured exaggeration—manufactured out of fear of a merger itself, notwithstanding the original enthusiasm for it.

3. We lost a second agency to the process. One of the original participants, a shelter for battered women, was affiliated with the Catholic Church. The arch-

bishop of the diocese noted that another of the entities was engaged in counseling the victims who came to it for help. In the many years of existence of the latter agency, there had not been a single instance where abortion had been "counseled." But, the archbishop insisted that each other entity sign a pledge that such would never occur *in the future*. The others felt that even though there was no propensity on their part to "counsel" abortion, they could not conscientiously sign such a pledge, and the shelter agency backed out. I remember vividly the passionate argument of a member of the shelter's board: This is not about abortion, it's about responding to domestic violence. Her argument was of no avail. She charged the diocese with jousting with windmills.

4. You will recall that one of the positive aspects of the project was the pledge on the part of the five EDs that no one of them would contend for the principal staff position in the merged agency. As I observed the project as it went forward, each seemed to conduct herself so as to carry out the pledge. But somehow, the one who was asked to send notices of the various meetings (of the EDs themselves and of the work group) was looked on by two of the others as trying to hog the limelight by so doing. That previous wonderful idealism began to lose its rosy glow.

5. Finally, a clash of cultures—the for-profit versus the nonprofit—killed all chances of a successful merger of the remaining three entities. It was the mindset of a trustee of one of the agencies, one of those successful businesspeople. He had "just been through a merger" of his own business venture and, by his own immodest admission, he knew "all about mergers in the business world." Unfortunately, he did not know *anything* about nonprofit organizations and

the requirement that they be open in all their dealings and make full disclosure of their conditions and
operations (except, of course for client/patient confidentiality). However, when it came time to cooper-
ate in the due diligence phase of the project, he refused to allow his ED to give substantial information
about his agency. After all, this dunderhead concluded, this would be "disclosing *trade secrets!*" No
amount of argument could persuade him that he
was in the wrong arena. He had no idea—and here's
a point for you to remember because it should per-
vade your thinking and be clearly communicated to
your board—that a nonprofit agency, vested with a
public trust, must operate openly in all respects,
open to all the world and to all inquiry.

I grieved a lot. But I learned a lot, too. Meanwhile, two of
the five agencies *did* survive the trauma and are now merrily
merged.

Let's get to something a bit easier to handle.

CHAPTER 8

Making Your Job Work Even Better

This chapter is mostly fun. It was for me, anyway. If you think your job as an ED is fair, try my job as a consultant some time. In this chapter we deal with how you handle a few less traumatic problems than those set forth in some of the other chapters. And for me, recalling some of my consultancies brings back smiles and chuckles. I always ask my client/audience to give me their written evaluations of the session. Usually they're quite favorable. But the most memorable one occurred last year in Minneapolis--100% of the respondents gave me an "outstanding", and as a bonus I received two marriage proposals.

LESSON 36—AVOID AN ADVISORY BOARD

My Favorite Alliteration

Your board, just like every other board in this world, will face a dilemma: What should it do about the trustee (let's use me as an example) whose term is about to expire? For the purposes of this lesson, we're going to assume that my term is not subject to renewal—either because of a specific provision in your bylaws, or because the decision not to renew results from your assessment process (Lesson 32). I refer to this as a dilemma, with its literal meaning of a problem that has two (or more) possible solutions, any one of which will help you muddle through but no one of which is *really* satisfactory. The board might look to you for suggestions.

You can suggest to the board that it offer to me a handshake and a pat on the back, or a commemorative brass plaque mounted on walnut for inclusion in my study, or a testimonial reception. Or you could attach my nameplate to a desk in the student lecture hall or to a gurney in the operating room or to a chair in the dress circle of the concert hall or to a pew in the sanctuary. Or, how about a heavy gold pocket watch with a cover over the face that snaps open obediently as you press the stem? I'd like that. If any of this sounds a bit frivolous to you, I want you to know that I recommend any of the above (or an equivalent) over the other, more usual, "solution." I refer, of course, to your agency putting me on an advisory board or committee, or an honorary board or committee, or an emeritus board or committee, *or a ceremonial group under any name*. Just *don't* do it.

Here again, we reach a supposed solution driven by that silly and misguided *warm, fuzzy* motivation. Sure, you like me and I've been a faithful, dedicated, and generous trustee on occasion. And more than that, you want me to continue the relationship and especially respond to all of the fundraising requests. I understand all of that. But in appointing me to any such group, your board starts down the primrose path. The decision will come to haunt the agency, and you in particular. Here are the hazards.

1.   If such a group has voting rights at the board table, you run the very risk that term non-renewal is designed to avoid. Here I am sitting at the board table with the same rights as if my term *had been renewed*, even though the assess-

ment process would have precluded me from being there. You'd be surprised at how frequently that happens just because the board wants to avoid hurting my feelings. The result can be a terminal case of "founder's disease."

2. If such a group is designed to be merely advisory or honorary in nature, that means that you, the staff, have still another level of folks to whom you must accommodate, to whom you must pay attention, to whom you must listen, and to whom you must account.

3. If my group is "advisory," how many times each year are you and the board chair going to call a meeting and get us together to seek our advice—really *seek* it? And how much information about the agency are you going to distribute to us, and how frequently? And once we give our advice and it isn't followed by the governing board itself, how soon before I realize that it's all been a charade anyway? And what happens to the agency's irrational hope that now, having discovered the charade, I'll continue to be generous? And what about staff time required to support and massage what has now become the equivalent of two boards?

4. If my group is merely "honorary," I get the charade picture even sooner. For I see that you're appointing to this honored group practically everybody who's leaving the board at the end of his or her term. Because it includes a lot of folks whom I disliked while I served with them (and naturally felt them to be much less worthy of the office than I was), I say to myself, "What's the big honor?"

Avoid all those headaches: Opt for the gold watch solution.

LESSON 37—SHOULD YOU BE A VOTING MEMBER OF YOUR BOARD?

I Vote *No*

In the annals of silly questions, this is one of the silliest. Yet it pops up all over. We can deal in a frivolity here, if we wish. Let's just say that we see no advantage to your having voting membership on the board—with one exception. If the issue is whether or not to discharge the ED, it won't get a unanimous vote. End of frivolity.

And yet, the issue crops up. I've seen it approached in a number of different ways, usually, but not always, by provision in the agency's bylaws. In one agency, there'll be a provision in the bylaws defining or describing your position and duties, with no mention of voting rights or provision for board membership. Here, clearly, you're not a member of the board. In another agency, you may be designated specifically as a board member with, or sometimes without, the right to vote. If you are given the right to vote, there may be some provision for you to recuse yourself if, of course, the issue involves you. In either case, the provision in your bylaw controls.

I have seen situations in which an ED wants to be a fully voting trustee, as well. I fail to see any validity to the reasoning of "it makes me feel an *equal* part of the group," "it gives me more influence with the board," "it gives me greater standing in the community," and so on.

This merely deals in redundancies. As ED, as the person who has (as we've mentioned frequently) the "immediate authority respecting every programmatic aspect of the agency's functioning," how can you be more "equal" than that? And as to "more influence with the board," if you do all that I tell you in this book—and I fully expect that you'll do just that—not only will you be the principal educator to the board, but you'll be making us exquisitely aware that you *are* our teacher, our mentor, our coach, and goodness knows what else. And we look to you for your guidance and advice and approval and approbation on almost every aspect of how we, the board, functions. How much more influence can you have, silly? As for "greater standing in the community," everyone knows that you're the one who makes the wheels go 'round. And when a trustee opens the door to a foundation or a donor, or whomever, he trots you out in front to make the "ask" or to give meaning to the presentation, and he arranges for you to make the speeches at the Rotary Club. For you to think that you are less than equal or less influential than a trustee is just an empty exercise in self-effacement. So I've made my point on *those* issues, but there's more.

Think about how you might diminish my feeling of good-will toward you if you insist on an at-the-board-table vote. If it's my resolution that's being considered, I fully expect that when the chair asks for your professional judgment before the vote, you'll present that judgment candidly and fearlessly. I shall, of course, respect your candor and courage even if you advise against the passage *of my proposal*. But if you have a vote and you actually *vote* against *me*, I shall probably be less understanding because in my mind, this involves your personal, not professional, judgment.

Don't get into that fix. It's not necessary.

Digression: This "equality" thing is really in the mind of the beholder. My father took the position that "one can be made to feel unequal only with his consent." I fell into the trap once, but came out of it with just a chuckle. It happened when I was asked to do a workshop on governance for the president and the board of a large southern university. I arrived on campus the night before the workshop was to convene, and I was invited to spend the night at the president's manor house. After a beer or two, the conversation became casual. The president, noting that my affiliation with higher education was "only" as a trustee, and that I was not to be paid for my consultancy, asked me why I was doing it. I responded that I have stars in my eyes when it comes to higher education, and that my consultancies allow me the privilege of meeting one-on-one with people in the exalted position of university president. I then added that that gives me a sense of honor and importance because under those circumstances, "they usually treat me like an equal" instead of just a lay person. The president's reply was this: "Lewis, if a university president treats you like an equal, you shouldn't be honored, you should be insulted." It works in all directions, doesn't it?

LESSON 38—TELL YOUR BOARD: IT'S *CARING* THAT COUNTS, NOT JUST CARE

Or, Am I Liable for That?

Many manuals for trustees specify certain "duties" of trusteeship. There are scores of versions of the issue, but most agree on two areas: the duty of loyalty and the duty of care. I'll be brief as to both, because this book is for you, the ED, not for them.

The "loyalty" thing relates to the board's need to adhere to the stated mission of the agency and not to meander about with its decisions based on, say, mere whim or faddish outside influences—sometimes called "flavor-of-the-month" decisions—or financial "opportunity." In other words, your trustees are enjoined from ignoring tradition in favor of a momentary advantage. Enough of that. But the second asserted "duty" intrigues me. It's that duty of "care."

That *sounds* appropriate enough, of course, in fact almost innocuous, but I find it a bit deceiving as purporting to represent a *real* duty for trustees. Here's why. It's usually pronounced in the context of using "care" so as not to run afoul of the law and thus invoke on oneself penalties or liability. And the law itself is very helpful on that score—in my mind, too helpful.

This all starts with the fact that:

1. Every one of the 50 states has some sort of set of statutory enactments respecting nonprofit agencies, how they are to be formed, and some of the rules relating to their internal governance, management, and operations.

2. Each set of statutes has a certain "spin" to it (I learned that word from the political world); the spin evolves from the legislative intent to *encourage* people to serve their communities by accepting membership on nonprofit boards, rather than to *discourage* them from doing so.

3. As a result, the statutes, in specifying the circumstances under which a trustee can be held personally liable or answerable for his or her actions *as* a trustee, impose a standard of "care" that is laughably low.

Although the language of the various state legislation varies, the sense is the same in all of the enactments. They provide in essence that a trustee acquits him- or herself of any such possible answerability or liability by acting "reasonably" or in "reasonable reliance" on his/her own judgment or on the reports, recommendations, or documents submitted to him/her. If that doesn't smack of a dilettantish approach to "care," I don't know what does. The problem, of course, is that the approach puts greater emphasis on "care" about making the trustees relatively immune for mistakes of judgment, even serious ones that harm the agency, than about "caring"—*really caring*—for the interests of the agency itself. But these statutes go even further in protecting the trustee. Most state legislation on the subject provides that the agency may indemnify a trustee against personal liability (for money damages, as an example, or for expenses for defense of a claim against him/her) if he's/she's sued for malfeasance or misfeasance as a trustee. The only exceptions, as I interpret them from my 46 years as a corporate lawyer, are those that constitute intentionally harming the agency or stealing from it. Thus, this additional level of insulation serves only to assure the trustee still further of a rather insidious byproduct of legislative intent—that "care" for the agency is certainly not the equivalent of "caring" for the interests of the agency, but more caring about one's own personal immunity. A "caring" interest equates with love for the agency, while care equates with acting defensively to avoid personal accountability. In effect, then, those indemnification statute enactments can encourage trustee misfeasance, malfeasance, and nonfeasance simply because (a) not only is it likely that the agency cannot get reimbursement for the trustee's non-caring , but (b) the agency also may have to reimburse (indemnify) that same trustee for costs incurred by him/her in defending any claim originating with such act of non-caring. Surely, Alice in Wonderland had a hand in that.

LESSON 39—MY LIFE AS A CONSULTANT TO NONPROFIT ORGANIZATIONS

What *You* Can Learn from It

As I meander through the golden years as an octogenarian, I reminisce, as you would suspect, on the twists and turns and cascade of events that, taken one at a time, make neither a sense nor a pattern. And not being a practitioner of any traditional religion, I blame what little *does* make sense on the intervention of two of my favorite deities—Zeus and Hera. They seem to have worked it out so that almost everything I've done earlier in life seems to "pay off" at some unrelated event later, sometimes much later. For example, during my vaudeville days as part of a kid act with my brother, I sang a song entitled "Lucky Lindy." This usually got a lot of applause from the audience, especially in the last week of May of 1927, when Charles Augustus Lindberg made his solo flight from New York to Paris. And it was popular for many months thereafter. My vaudeville career ended in 1931, but I never forgot the lyrics. And 69 years after that, at the wedding of the last of our five children—a girl this time—I sang it once more at the wedding dinner and enjoyed a standing ovation and three encores of the chorus, the last two of which were joined in by the guests. The point that I make here is that everything that happens in life on a particular day is "grist for the mill" for all your days thereafter. So that's one thing for *you* to learn from *my* experience. A perfect example of this arose when a few years ago, I went to California to do a two-day retreat workshop for a university president and her board of trustees.

My telling of the story requires going back in time to the fall of 1936. When I fell into the pattern of life as a 16-year-old freshman at Hamilton College, I could not have dreamed that my life there on campus at that time would someday affect my performance as a consultant to the leadership—ED and board—of L. University, a church-related institution. It all started with my yearning to be admitted to Hamilton: I had read the college catalog from cover to cover dozens of times. I was naive, and some of what I read made no sense to me. In retrospect, my naiveté was laughable. For example, I thought the word "orientation" had something to do with Chinese literature, which, at the time, held no interest for me. "Matriculation" was a mystery to me. And some course descriptions had me puzzled, especially the references in the science areas: histology and physical chemistry. But my frequent reading of the catalog had me to the point where I actually memorized some of its descriptive passages. One particular passage appeared on the first page, right after the proud announcement of the founding of the institution in 1789. "Hamilton College, while non-sectarian, is a distinctly Christian institution." Coming from Jewish parentage, I suspected that this *might* possibly have some effect on my life at college, but I was uncertain as to exactly what would happen. I soon learned.

Those days were different—the middle 1930s—and college rules were college rules and were to remain unquestioned. Minorities were inured to the idea that they were minorities, and that most rules were made by and for the majority. And if the college rule required students to attend daily morning chapel at which Christian hymns were sung and prayers were recited, students, even Jewish students, sang the songs and mouthed the prayers. So that became part of my daily routine. And I attended faithfully every morning during my four academic years.

The scene now shifts, many years later, to a gorgeous resort in Palm Springs, California, where my two-day consulting retreat was to be held. I had never been to Palm Springs before, and the taxi driver must have thought me insane as I broke into gales of laughter at the street names: John Wayne Avenue, Frank Sinatra Boulevard, and Fred Waring Street. Such high cultural icons!

When I reached my assigned room, a recorded message on my telephone invited me to "come to worship" in room 109 at eight o'clock the following morning, before my first session was to begin. I arrived at 109 just as the person at the podium (I later learned that she was the president of the university) was asking the organist to begin playing the morning hymn. She saw me and beckoned me to an empty seat in the front row of the room. I arrived at my seat just a moment before the gathering stood to sing the hymn. In plain sight of everyone there, a young man in the next seat graciously offered me his hymnal and I, *ungraciously,* held up my two hands in an apparent sign of rejection, whereupon he kept his hymnal. When worship was over, the president called me to the podium, introduced me in terms that were too glowing, and asked me to say a few words. I could not get the incident of the hymnal out of my mind, so I decided to address the issue.

"I assume that you all saw my ungracious gesture of response when my neighbor there offered me his hymnal. Please do not misinterpret it. Although I come from a different religious background than yours, I must tell you about the role of Christian hymns in my life." I then told them about my life at college, particularly the chapel part. I then continued. "I refused the hymnal only because I didn't need it to join you in the singing. You see, not only do I know every hymn in your hymnal, but I know all four-part harmonies to every hymn in your hymnal—first tenor, second tenor, baritone, and bass.

The audience reaction was warm and affectionate. ED, you never know when "it"—whatever the "it" is—will come in handy. Oh yes, I was invited to lead worship the next morning, but I declined, reminding myself of an old vaudeville adage: Always leave them wanting more.

LESSON 40—WANTED: *TOUGHNESS*

More on my Life as a Consultant

Here's the lesson to be learned by you from this, another of *my* experiences as a consultant. There are times when you, the ED, must be direct with your board about demanding that it play its governance role. If you cannot do so, then as a last result, you may have to engage an outside consultant to help you do it. Talk this over with your board chair if necessary—he may be having the same problem. But the lesson, stated in other terms, is that there may be times to use the "tough love" approach.

This involved my assignment by the people at the Association of Governing Boards of Universities and Colleges (AGB). I was to conduct a two-day retreat for the board and president of a private, freestanding university in a midwestern state. The subject was to be "board accountability." It was a critical time in my life: My cardiac records were being evaluated at the Cleveland Clinic to determine if, and how soon, I might need open-heart surgery. The decision had not yet been made by the time I left home for the retreat.

The evening before the first day of the event, I had dinner alone with the president. He complained about his board, saying they were a passive bunch. He said that they acted as a rubber stamp for his recommendations and decisions, never asking him to justify or defend his position on anything. They seemed to be content with just coming to the quarter-annual board meetings, enjoying the pleasant campus environment, attending some carefully arranged social events, and going home. You might think, of course, that such a situation would make him the happiest university president in the world. But he was too sophisticated for that. He felt unchallenged and, more important, the board did not operate in a governance role. The board was just going through the formal ministrations of governance, but mandating neither direction nor vision. He feared that if he were suddenly out of the picture, the board would not take hold of the issues to be addressed and the university would drift along on automatic pilot. He hoped that I, as an outsider, could help. He reasoned that I could say things about board accountability that, coming from him, would be resented.

The next morning, the process began after we all met at breakfast. During the morning session, my presentation was received with far less attention and enthusiasm than the board secretary's announcement about the lunch menu. It was the same in the afternoon session, during which the announcement about the dinner menu and the evening's entertainment got top billing and a better reception than my stuff. At about 4 P.M., in the middle of my presentation on accountability, the yawning of the audience was interrupted. I was called off the podium to a telephone in the next room: "It's your wife." Joanne was calling to tell me that the day after my return home, I was scheduled for quadruple bypass surgery. This unwelcome news gave me a startling new sense of mortality and the determination to use my remaining moments to say what in my mind had to be said.

I was thinking in terms of trusteeship as my only remaining, and most precious, client after 46 years in law practice. I then thought about the fact that this audience of trustees, by its passivity and lack of caring about and dedication to this 126-year-old university, was making a mockery of it. So when I got back on the platform, and after a few introductory sentences, I told them just that. And then I embellished by saying (this is almost verbatim):

"I suggest that you reconsider continuing your affiliation with this university. I assume that you accepted membership on this board because its mission represented a high priority for you and the type of world you like to envision. So now, think about it this way: If the mission of this university occupies a place lower than the third romance in your life—just behind your family and your mode of earning a living—just resign from the board."

There was a low groan and the nervous shifting of bodies in the chairs. We went on with process for the rest of that day and half of the next day. Then I flew home to my bypass surgery. It was generally successful, but Zeus and Hera punished me for my pomposity in front of those trustees. I regained my senses in the middle of the surgery and had no way of communicating that fact to the surgical team. I also encountered hepatitis, a urinary infection, nightmares in revisiting scenes of World War II combat, and sleep deprivation. As to those last two, it was either sleeping and having the nightmares, or not sleeping at all. I solved the dilemma by watching the shopping channel all night long.

There's a sequel to the "telling off" incident. Some weeks later, the president told me that he had received a communication from one of his trustees. She made it clear that Lewis had offended her deeply, but had influenced her thinking about trusteeship and how she had not assumed her real role. And that in acknowledgement, she was sending him this "token" of regret—a six-figure contribution to the capital campaign.

I can't guarantee that result every time. But it's sure worth the risk of taking your trustees to the woodshed once in a while.

LESSON 41—STILL MORE ON A CONSULTANT'S LIFE, BUT FOR FUN ONLY

You Won't Learn Anything from This

I used to do a lot of mentor-type consultancies for AGB and I enjoyed all of them—meeting nice people in the non-profit higher education field (presidents and trustees), all with varying degrees of dedication to the cause. Some of the experiences were more pleasant than others. This sometimes depended on how hospitably they treated me. My first such experience was a downer. But let me tell you about four entirely different ones.

Experience 1

Imagine a small college in the wilds of Wyoming, where the president invited his board and me for dinner one night and the menu included bear meat from an animal that he had hunted down a few weeks before. I actually liked the meal; that was a success. But the opening mentoring session the next morning started out as a flop. I used an introductory device that I copied from someone else. The trustees were arrayed around a table, flanking the president. I started to my left, telling the group that I was calling on each one to tell me what he (there were no she's there that day) expected to get out of the sessions, so I could design the presentation accordingly. The first response: "I'm just a pharmacist and I'd like to know more about the board's role versus the president's role." *Bingo* for me—exactly what I had prepared to cover. The next response: "I'm an accountant and new to the board. Please tell us what we should be doing about planning the college's future." Another bingo, and a key part of what the mentor usually brings up for discussion. Then the fatalistic third response. I should have suspected trouble, because this trustee identified himself as a rancher and his twang was a lot twangier than that of the first two. "You asked me what I expect out of the sessions. I don't expect to get anything out of them. In fact, I wonder why you're here." In my naiveté, and being miffed and surprised and embarrassed, I answered him on a literal basis, thinking that I would carry the day.

Me: You should know that I'm here because your board adopted a formal resolution, a copy of which I have right here, inviting me to *be* here.

He: Oh yes, I know about that. But *you* should know that *I* voted against the resolution.

I should like to report to you that he and I got along a lot better after that dialogue, but the fact is that we didn't.

Experience 2

This is one where I knew in advance that I would probably not be treated like a visiting dignitary. It started with a call from a gentleman with a magnificent southern drawl. He identified himself as the special assistant to the president of C. University, in a southern state, and asked if I could do a two-day workshop/retreat for the university board and president. He named a particular set of days that were clear on my professional calendar (I was still a practicing lawyer), but I told him that I'd have to check my family calendar. I called him the following day to report my availability, and here was the surprising colloquy.

He (very drawly): That's fine. I'll write you a letter verifying the arrangements.

Me: I'll look forward to receiving your letter.

He: You know, Lewis, you and I have something in common.

Me (knowing it was not the drawl, and not being very interested anyway): Oh.

He: Yes. I'm a lawyer, too, but I was never in the private practice of law.

Me: Oh.

He: You see, I was the Judge Advocate General of the Navy under President Nixon.

Me (with all the enthusiasm I could muster at the mention of Nixon's name): Oh.

He (getting the point and deciding to change the subject): Lewis, you sound like a fine gentleman. How about our getting together on a less formal basis? May I call you by your first name?

Me: Certainly. Most people call me Robert.

He: Good. "Robert" it is.

Me: Should this informality be reciprocal?

He: Sure.

Me: Then what shall I call you?

He: Admiral!

Experience 3

Here's another one. This was fun all the way, and ended nicely. Another call started it all and it was a request for my services as a consultant to him and his board—a two-day retreat.

He: My name is _____ and I'm the president of _____college in eastern Pennsylvania. (He gave the name of a college with the same name as that of a hill in central Italy, somewhere between Arezzo and Assisi. By coincidence, I knew the name of the hill from my artillery days in World War II). Have you ever heard of my college?

Me: No, but I know the name because of its association with Saint Francis.

He: How do you explain that?

Me: Well, sir, although I'm of a different faith, St. Francis is one of my heroes and I know a lot about him.

He: What about the hero part?

Me: I admire anyone who was so devout and driven by such deep faith.

He: Interesting, Lewis. He's a hero of mine, too.

Me: But there's another basis for my admiration.

He: Tell me what that is.

Me: You see, I have a warped sense of humor. And another aspect of my admiration for St. Francis was because he was nutty as a fruitcake. He went around talking to flowers, but never got a response. Then he tried birds, also without success. Finally he tried animals, even the ferocious ones that then populated the hills of Tuscany, again without success. Then one day as he was walking up our hill, he kneeled down to pray and finally received his answer in the form of the stigmata. What a triumph for faith.

He: There's a coincidence here. My college is owned by the Sisters of St. Francis and my board is composed of 27 nuns.

Me: There's nothing that would please me more than to spend two days in a retreat with 27 nuns.

And so I went and had one of the more gratifying retreat experiences of my career. The sisters were attentive, participatory, unnecessarily respectful, and ever pleasant. As we made our way through the process, I became increasingly enthusiastic with our achievements and, as is the case with me on such occasions, increasingly loud in my delivery. It's not pomposity, really, it's just plain enthusiasm when I'm working with a group of trustees who "get it." But as you'll see, I guess that I was *really* loud.

The night before I was to leave the college—we had already finished the retreat—the president, the sisters, and I were having a wonderful wine-charged dinner at a huge round table in the great refectory. Toward the end of the meal—and I'll tell you the first part only because there was a second part—one of the sisters announced in lovely tones:

Professor Lewis, during your time here with us, we have learned about your humane and humanitarian interests. The other sisters and I want you to know that we think you represent the core values of the Franciscans; do you know what they are?

Me: Yes, sister, I do. And I have never felt so honored in my life. Tomorrow I'm going to go directly home and tell my family that I represent the core values of the Franciscans.

(At this point, there was a loudly voiced interjection from the Mother Superior.)

She: Save *one*, Professor Lewis.

Me: What is that, Mother?

She: We all think that you had better work on your humility!

Experience 4

Here's another fun one that has little do with your education as an ED. But here's the way I figure it: There's room for fun in every life. If I wished to put this in the form of a lesson, I'd entitle it "Having the Last Word."

This was a military college for which I was doing the usual two-day president/board retreat at a beautiful spa somewhere in the Adirondacks. If I were easily intimidated by relative rank, I, who took five laborious years of wartime military service to progress from private to first lieutenant, would have been reduced to blubber by the array of higher ranks that confronted me. The president was a retired major general and the board members were all of equal rank or higher. The exception was two women, each of whom was an admiral in the Navy. My walk to the podium after the president's morning introduction was interrupted by a tug at my sleeve. When I stopped to respond to the "tugger," who still held my sleeve, he leaned over to me and whispered this rather startling greeting: "Lewis, if you're here to straighten out our board, forget it. We like the board just the way it is...*understand ?!*" As he gripped my arm ever more tightly, I understood. Not a propitious start.

The rest of the morning turned out a lot better, with good conversation and a lot of participation on the part of most of the audience, rank aside. There was one notable exception—a stern-looking ramrod type. He never changed his expression or moved in his seat during the entire three hours of the morning session and the two hours of the afternoon part. It was strange. I recognized his face as one that I had seen before, but I could not relate it to time or place. After dinner that night, the president invited me and a few of the trustees to the spa's tavern for some imbibing. We sat at a large round table and just blabbed. Soon, the man with the stone face appeared, looked us over, and said "Thanks, I shall" in response to the president's invitation to join us. He sat directly across from me: I stared at him for a few seconds, and then the epiphany!

Me: Are you General George S. Patton, Jr.?

He: Yes, I am. (He forced a slight smile, and seemed to relax.)

Me (encouraged, and wanting to be friendly): Sir, I knew your father.

He (now with real interest): You did?

Me: Yes, and I shall never forget my conversation with him.

He: Will you tell me about it?

Me: Sure. It was July of 1943, in the port of Licata, Sicily, two days after the beginning of the Allied invasion of the island. Your father was commander of the operation.

He: Yes, I know. But what about the conversation?

Me: Well, sir, it was brief and to the point. Your father came speeding along the sea road in his command car, stopped within yards of me, looked at me parked at the side of the road, and called out to me, "Lieutenant, get that goddamn jeep out of there, my tanks are coming through!" And I said, "Yes. Sir!" And that was our conversation. It felt good getting in the last word.

LESSON 42—TIME OUT

Time for a Bit of Ranting and Raving

It's all very discouraging. My advice here will surprise you: Stay away from every event that advertises itself as a national workshop or forum on nonprofit leadership. You're bound to be bombarded by that brand of mindless political correctness that's peculiar to the nonprofit world, just the kind of stuff that I've been warning you against—you know, trying to create a lovey-dovey relationship between board and staff. But lately it's getting worse, trying to create the illusion that for-profits and nonprofits aren't really that different, and that each can learn a lot from the other. At this moment, I'm looking at a flyer highly touting exactly that very type of national forum and a dozen or so breakout sessions on aspects of leadership. Zounds! I'm in a foul mood. Here are a few examples of why—the pap that could divert us from pursuing our goal of understanding the realities of the nonprofit world.

Example 1

The first involves "Improving the Bottom Line: Board Changes Lead to Organizational Success." And after all I've told you in Lessons 31 and 32! I'll elaborate just for emphasis. A nonprofit agency has no bottom line. The "bottom line" is a mere mathematical number in the operating statement of a for-profit agency, that has, for that agency, a magical importance. It is the primary measure of its success or failure, quite irrespective of that agency's methods of operation or possible adverse effect on the environment or possible insensitive employment practices. If the bottom line is black, the for-profit is considered a success. If the bottom line is red, it's a failure. That simple criterion properly applies to the for-profit agency, a completely different organization with which a nonprofit agency should not be compared. The fact that a nonprofit agency is operating at a deficit is not a necessary indication of its worthiness to exist or to merit support. Very few nonprofit agencies can achieve through their own income streams (fees for service, admission charges, dues, and the like) more than one-half of their operating costs. So, if a bottom-line criterion were to be used, we'd all be considered unworthy. (We have a board of trustees to assure us of making up the difference so that we can go on toward fulfilling our mission.) *Mission!* That's our bottom line, not a number. The type of session to which I'm referring here will have executives from both sectors rubbing each other's backs, twisting truth and logic, and misleading the audience away from the fact that for-profits and nonprofits simply have different, ever so different, *souls*. And as to learning from each other—ridiculous! The only thing the for-profits can teach us is to worship at the wrong shrine—where financial success is the sole criterion for existence—just the opposite of where our thoughts should be. Conversely, the only thing we can teach the for-profits is altruism and humanism, neither of which will assure them of the profits they seek.

Example 2

The second charade that masquerades as a training session is entitled "Enhancing the Board/Chief Executive Officer Partnership." Just go back to Lesson 15 on this bit of illusion. Let's get it straight, ED: You the ED and I the board are *not* partners, dammit! We've already specified the definition of a partnership as applying to an arrangement between (say) two people, neither one of whom is subordinate to the other. Here goes that touchy-feely rubbish again. Those panelists who seem to think that every human relationship has to be touchy-feely to work well have taken sway in the "forum" world. Next time you go to one of those sessions, boo them off the stage. Nothing that I write here is intended to degrade you or your importance to me and our agency. But you, my dear ED, are subordinate to me, definitely subordinate. Our areas of authority are on a different level, but your station is lower than mine. I don't care to put it in more palatable terms because the reality is that I have the final say on everything. I have the ultimate authority. I have the right to overrule your every decision relating to our agency (if I'm courageous or stupid enough to want to do so). You can't do that with my decisions. Subject to any contractual arrangements between us, I have the authority to terminate your position with the agency. You can't do that to me. How can it be said that neither of us is subordinate to the other? This all comes about because our colleagues in our world just don't like the idea that sometimes we have tension between us that arises out of turf wars or differences in opinion or just plain personal dislike. So what do they do? They call us "partners," which we aren't. If there must be a label, let them call us "colleagues." This stems from the Latin, "co" [together] and "lego" [deputize], and describes our role and relationship perfectly. It means that we are the two (in this case) people who are appointed or deputized to achieve a result. Of course we have the same ambition—the achievement of our agency's mission. But we pursue the two different avenues of leadership to help the agency get there—governance and management. It's nice if we don't ever have a turf war or if we forever like each other, but that's not the reality and we shouldn't be "taught" that it is. And as for differences in opinion, that, after all, makes for good decisions, so we should encourage it. Pollyannas, get off the podium!

Example 3

The third session, which could possibly be the most insidious of all, is entitled "The Grantmaker's Seat at the Board Table." In this connection, I refer you to the stuff we covered in Lesson 30, dealing with the numerous "stakeholders" of our agency. We recognized the vast number of categories of people and organizations that can claim to be stakeholders in our agency's functioning, and that our board table decisions should not be made without considering whether, and to what extent, their collective and respective stakes should be weighed in the balance. We noted that our agency's institutional funders (foundations) do have a stake, just by virtue of having encouraged us with financial support. Well, this scheduled session deals with the ever-growing trend of allowing the grantmaker a voting seat at the board table. Let's look at this outrage.

There was a time when I was able to tell my graduate school classes at the Mandel Center for Nonprofit Organizations at Case Western Reserve University—students who aspire to be the future EDs—that if you have an agency that represents a good idea for helping alleviate a community need, it'll be funded. But that is no longer the case. The first step in the change came about when the foundations themselves decided to be proactive, rather than just passively receiving and deciding on the proposals for funding coming their way. Their own missions became more specific. Instead of offering, as they once did, open-ended support for a virtuous agency dedicated to the problems of, say, domestic violence, they decided that the more critical needs lay in, say, education or health care or substance abuse, or whatever. Consequently, we saw the growth of foundation "guidelines" that, in effect, made it clear as to where they were going to put their money. All others stay out.

Let's assume that our agency has found an institutional donor and our mission fits its guidelines. But now, under the guise of that donor wanting to see "increased accountability" on our part, it asks for voting membership on our board. I'll give you the money if you put me on your board (that trade-off is exactly what we're taking about here). The conflict of interest is clear. It's no different from our other examples of "constituency representation"—the professor on the university board, medical staff on the hospital board. And what about the needy and worthy nonprofit that doesn't fit within the guidelines? Is our great world now to be influenced by that cynically altered golden rule: He who has the gold, rules?

Does this device mean that the rest of us at the board table are so cowed by the funder's largesse that we are now sub-servient to its mission without necessary regard to our own?

I leave to you the answers to those questions. But here again, we deal with trends that sneak their way into the non-profit world and despoil our purity of purpose.

CHAPTER 9

Inside the Life of the Nonprofit

This is what the concept of our nonprofit world is all about. I hope that it can stay this way. Will you help me "see to it that" it will? I'm counting on you. We need good organizational (governance) documents, the right motivation, and the downright purity of purpose.

LESSON 43—GOVERNANCE DOCUMENTS

Where Life (Nonprofit Life, That is) Begins

When I resigned from the practice of law, I lost the privilege of giving legal advice, so I won't do so here. There are enough books and manuals and lawyers around to tell you what steps you must take if, starting from scratch, you want to create a nonprofit agency. My only advice to you in that connection is that you *do* engage a lawyer to accompany you down that path until you have (a) properly incorporated your agency in the state in which you plan to have your principal operations, and (b) gone through the steps required by law to achieve your "501 (c)(3)" status. There is no good substitute for sound legal advice and guidance as you go through each such procedure. So get it. It's not an easy do-it-yourself task.

Here's the usual scenario and it starts with (a) above. The founders of the agency, enthusiastic about their newly developed idea for a home for runaway girls, take the first step. With help from counsel, they file with the secretary of state of their particular state a formal document called articles of incorporation (certificate of incorporation in some states).

Articles of Incorporation ("Articles")

This is usually a sketchy document requiring only the corporate name, the place of its principal office, its "purpose" clause, and the names and addresses of those persons who will be its initial trustees. The articles may contain other, more detailed provisions, but there's a caveat here, the first of many that I'll insert throughout this lesson.

Caveat: For example, the articles *may* include even minor administrative provisions, such as those dealing with a quorum at meetings, which are normally included in the agency's code of regulations (see *infra*). I recommend against including such a minor provision in the articles because if later it should be decided to amend that provision, the amendment requires a separate formal filing with the secretary of state. Otherwise, if it's in the code of regulations, the amendment can be accomplished internally.

The purpose clause is usually an expression of the incorporators' first thoughts as to what, eventually, will be identified as the agency's mission.

Caveat: Here is one of the realities as to initial organizational documents: They are frequently composed in haste and with the paramount need to comply, probably minimally, with the legal steps required just to bring the organization into existence. The purpose clause may or may not become the agency's actual mission statement used thereafter, say, for example, in its 501 (c)(3) filing with the Internal Revenue Service or in its institutional plan or in its fundraising case statement or its other agency documents. The trend toward making these later refinements is particularly noticeable with respect to the agency's code of regulations, a discussion of which follows.

Code of Regulations ("Code")

Most states allow the incorporators to create a code, sometimes carelessly called "bylaws," that defines the organizational structure of the agency. This represents the opportunity for the founders to legislate, internally, all of the rules, policies, practices, and other details pertaining to any and every aspect of governance, management, and operations. Here again, there is the tendency in many cases to put together a document based on borrowed forms of boilerplate just to "cover the bases." The provisions could include matters as broad as a statement of policy (the procedure for handling conflicts of interest at the board level), or as narrow, and silly, as the requirement of the signature of two officers on all agency checks in excess of $100.

For purposes of assigning to you still more leadership responsibility, I'm going to simplify our scenario. I'm going to assume that your employment with your agency begins sometime *after* its articles have been filed and its initial code has been established. It will be incumbent on you, then, to arrange for a review of the code so that you can avoid the pitfalls that I'm describing in these caveats. We shall not deal with each of the scores of provisions

that make their way into the code, only the possible trou-
blemakers.

1.   *Number of trustees:* The code may provide for flexibil-
ity by specifying a minimum number and a maxi-
mum number, to be determined by the board from
time to time. I'm frequently asked about the ideal
size for a board. The answer is just what you'd expect: It depends. But even though there is no one-
size-fits-all rule, there are indeed parameters. It
should be large enough to accommodate the needs
for (a) adequate diversity that reflects the profile of
the community served by the agency, and (b) sufficient membership to serve as officers of the board
and on its various committees. Yet, once the diversity issue is satisfied, it should be small enough to
act efficiently and effectively as a consultative, deliberative body. If one must err to one side or the other,
I suggest that you err on the side of being too small.
The worst that might happen is that the trustees
may be overworked—not such a terrible fate. But to
err on the side of being too large has its more significant hazards.

Caveat: One nonprofit agency for which I refused to accept a
consultancy has 127 trustees on its board. Many are *ex officio*
by reason of holding public office (I don't remember whether
or not the vice president of the United States is one of them),
or by reason of being trustees of other organizations in the geographic vicinity. How does this stack out? First, a board of
127 trustees is not a board, it's a gang—completely unwork-
able, completely incapable of acting efficiently and effectively
as a consultative deliberative body. Second, inevitably, a
board that's too big (even half that big is too big) develops its
own "inner board" of a few people who bravely attend some
meetings and muddle through toward making some decisions. Third, it's virtually impossible for you, the ED, to attend to the important programmatic business of the agency if

you're trying to corral 127 people for the periodic meetings of board and committees. I was amused when I attended a social engagement that was attended, also, by two members of that board. One asked the other why he hadn't been attending the board meetings of the "X Circle Development Corporation." The answer was, "I didn't know that I'm a member of that board, too." How's that for fulfilling the public trust?

2.   *Quorum:* The code will provide for the proportion or number of trustees who must be present at a meeting in order to constitute a quorum—the condition for having a valid meeting at which action can be taken. Some states specify that a certain percentage of trustees, sometimes a majority of those serving, is required as a quorum. Others allow *any* number to qualify as a quorum.

Caveat: If too great a proportion is required, it may be difficult to assemble a valid meeting, especially in an agency where trustee enthusiasm is low. If too small a number of trustees is required—say, a mere majority of the fifteen trustees serving—then the presence of seven of the fifteen present will allow the meeting to go forward and, unless otherwise specifically provided, four of the seven can make the agency's board-level decisions. That may be what you want; then again it may not be.

3.   *Defining authority:* This is a bit tricky because it involves terminology. Most codes use language that, in effect, vests in the board of trustees "all of the capacity and authority of the corporation." This is a clear statement of the board having (we've stated it so many times in this book) the "ultimate" authority. But as the provision comes down to us in other forms, we find such statements as "the board of trustees shall *manage* the affairs of the corporation," and that pronouncement immediately raises the question of where you, the ED and thus the pur-

ported manager, stand in the life of the agency. It can get worse. I've seen this. First, the head of the board is referred to as the "president" of the agency, not as the "chairperson." That is then followed by referring to the president as the "chief executive officer" of the agency.

Caveat: These types of provisions spell potential disaster for you as the *real chief executive officer* in whom there should be vested the *real authority to manage the affairs of the corporation.* These provisions reflect an institutional mindset that belies your claim to your rightful share of the agency's leadership. The person who "chairs" the board should not be referred to as "president," a term that clearly equates with executive management and causes confusion with your title as ED.

4. *More on "authority" issues:* The code should be the instrument that clarifies issues of authority and responsibility rather than blurring that much needed clarity. It doesn't always work that way. I refer to the code that was hastily drafted without necessary thought as to the operational effect of some of its provisions. First, let's deal with what I call a mindset problem related to "authority." It involves the terminology used to describe the governing board. The people who serve on boards of nonprofit agencies are called by different names: directors, trustees, regents, visitors, overseers, and probably others.

Caveat: If indeed we're identifying the title of those people who serve on the governing board of a nonprofit agency and we want to characterize that authority, I opt for the exclusive use of the term "trustees." The word implies exactly what society expects of such people—to accept the responsibility for the resources *entrusted* to them, to use those resources as a *public trust* for the benefit of the community, and to be accountable to the community for its performance. The overtone of all of that is the accountability that we demand of people in such positions. The most frequently used alternative term is "directors," and the differences are immediately apparent. That term smacks of the for-profit world and the people who sit on its boards, with none of the overtones of that essential element of trust in the sense that I've described. Directors of for-profits are expected to do some actual directing, of course, but are primarily expected to produce a profit without any necessary regard to community welfare or humane response to the human needy. I am not suggesting that directors, just by virtue of that name, will be less effective at the board table than their counterpart trustees. But I am saying that there's the possibility of a mindset that ignores the soul of trusteeship that derives from the very term "trustee." The other terms such as regent, visitor, or overseer are just fancy fronts.

Then there's the question of specific authority. Although indeed the code is the place to decide on detailed allocation of authority, some provisions can be barriers to operational or managerial efficiency.

Caveat: I refer here to provisions that go against the very spirit of the division of leadership turf that, although sometimes fuzzy, is nonetheless an issue to be respected. This is always a one-way street; it's the board jumping the fence into your inarguable area. "All checks in an amount exceeding $100 must have two authorized signatures and board approval." Although this sounds like the epitome of fiscal prudence, the ripple effects are ludicrous. If you're one of the authorized signatories, it requires you to keep the second one constantly in your sight if bills are to be paid in a timely manner. (Or do you just do what happens in most cases with such a requirement—one of you signs a whole stack of checks in blank and in advance?) And as to the "board approval" part, do we really want the board agenda to be weighted down with the renewal of the typewriter lease, the roster of regular compensation checks to our 27 employees, and the bill from the printer for envelopes and stationery? Yet I see this so frequently. Equally frequently I see this: "The personnel committee of the board shall approve all staff hiring." Don't stand for it! The staff is your exclusive turf. If you are to have total responsibility for the efficient and effective functions of management, any trustee-level intrusion compromises your control, hence your authority, hence a fair opportunity to judge *your* effectiveness.

Heads up EDs! This is a special announcement. Up until now, you've endured 43 lessons, each one pertaining to the leadership that's demanded of you as the professional head of your agency. Now that you're warmed up to the process, I'm going to take you through four situations/scenarios, each of which requires of you an extra something. It might be an extra measure of forcefulness, diplomacy, understanding, tolerance—or a combination of all of those. Ready?

LESSON 44—MOTIVATING YOUR BOARD

It Is Your Job To Do

We've been covering a lot of material up 'til now, and it's mostly about *you, your* duties, and *your* responsibilities. I hope that you're getting the point that the success of *your* nonprofit organization depends primarily on the extent to which *you* perform *your* role. I hope also that you note the emphasis on the second person singular in those previous two sentences. We've already established that you're the principal educator to your board (Lesson 6), but "that's only the beginning, folks, only the beginning." (Remember those ringing words from Cap'n Andy in Jerome Kern's "Showboat"? Or are you too young?) It now continues.

Educating your board to its role and accountabilities is just the first part. Now you have to deal with something that doesn't go by the rules: *actually **motivating** your board to fulfill that role and assume its accountabilities.* This simply means infusing into an otherwise casual or hesitant board a real enthusiasm for the task at hand. Here's where your leadership (Lesson 21) is put to the test. I've already concluded that that quality can't be taught, but I can be helpful in suggesting to you a fourfold approach for exercising your leadership skills and achieving the desired result. It begins with the board chair and whatever enhancements you can add to strengthen that benign conspiracy that we've described in Lesson 4. It ends with him, too.

Step 1: The Board Chair

Once you have his attention on the matter, get his approval and support for the basic theme that must underlay any successful attempt at motivating a board: "The Real Role of the Board in the Life of the Nonprofit Organization." That role must be restated before it can be enthusiastically endorsed. Tell him that the theme, once agreed on between the two of you, must be followed up by a session with the board as a whole as well as individual sessions with each trustee, and that he himself must play a significant role in both. Those are the next steps, and I'm going to suggest the scenarios and even some of the dialogue.

Step 2: The Board

Arrange for a few well-publicized occasions to emphasize that trusteeship is not a casual arrangement between the agency and a group of volunteers (Lesson 3). Have the chair deliver an appropriate introduction specifying that a basic, implied policy of every nonprofit agency is to identify "The Real Role of the Board in the Life of the Nonprofit Organization," and that *this* agency is going to emphasize that theme during your (and his) tenure. He should explain that experience discloses that a nonprofit agency flourishes in its attempt at accomplishing mission in direct relation to how well a board understands that real role. He will then state that he has asked you to elaborate on the basics of that theme.

You must then describe it as ownership, control, responsibility, and accountability. It must be described further as a position of trust and honor in the community. It must be described still further as so important as a hunk of the humanity that's so desperately needed in the world—as so essential to the welfare of the community—as to represent the trustees' third full-time commitment (first being family, second being mode of earning a living, and third being this organization). The clear implication of the message should be, perhaps in gentler terms than I'm now suggesting, that unwillingness to accept these terms equates with resignation. To paraphrase Shakespeare's Hamlet, "The *mindset's* the thing."

Step 3: Each Individual Trustee

Depending on the size of the board, in the course of your tenure with the agency, you should arrange to meet with each trustee periodically. That's just good sense. But for now, we're referring to the first meeting with each of them after the whole-board meeting just described. Have the chair at each such meeting so that he can have the benefit of the thoughts and wisdom that evolve from them. (This leads to Step 4 in the process.) Ask each trustee (a) why he/she agreed to become a board member; (b) what he/she is doing to support the agency's objectives; (c) what his/her preferences are as to committee service; (d) the extent to which his/her service to date has been satisfying, disappointing, stimulating, boring, or whatever; and (e) how his/her enthusiasm might be kindled, rekindled, or enhanced.

Step 4: The Board Chair Again

Now we're going back into our benign conspiracy. You and the board chair should discuss the situation as to each trustee, concentrating on how his/her interests and energies can be exploited so as to enhance motivation. You will decide between the two of you who will play what part in this very focused phase of trustee development. The chair must be reminded that he is the disciplinarian of the board, not you. Thus, he must be the one to follow up on such matters as committee assignments, financial contributions, meeting attendance, and the like. You, on the other hand, will follow up on reminding each trustee of the agency's role in answering the deficiencies in a needy community. You will decide on these strategies in this benign conspiracy session.

We are now past the matter of merely telling the trustee his/her role. We are at the issue of moving that trustee to an emotional state of wanting to see that role fulfilled.

This whole area of "motivation" is one in which the skillful personal touch is essential. It's something you can't buy or borrow.

LESSON 45—GETTING YOUR STAFF "ON BOARD"

Bringing the Parts Together: Your Job

The scenario here is a college campus and you're the president. I'm part of the on-site visiting team looking into the matter of re-accreditation. I take advantage of the privilege of interviewing your subordinate staff members and I mention your board of trustees. The likely reaction is a smile, a smirk, a snicker, or a rolling-back of the eyes—hardly any one of them a gesture of admiration. That's unfortunate. I don't contend that a board of trustees deserves, *ex officio (Latin:* just by virtue of the office) automatic admiration, or even automatic respect. However, just as important as it is for the board to understand its own real role, it is equally important that the other constituencies of the agency know it as well.

As part of my assignment, I ask those staff people at the college for comments on the board. I also ask them for comments on themselves, faculty, students, the football team, and the college store. But mention of the board gets a more emotional treatment: two extremes, both of which are denigratic and self-contradictory. "They're always meddling in my area without knowing anything about it," or "We never see them. It's as if they don't exist. They never ask me anything. Then every once in a while they make some decision from on high affecting lots of lives, but without knowing what they're doing." The likelihood is that neither of those extremes is accurate, that each is a misperception, but they're perceptions nonetheless and each is a problem for you, my president, to address.

Because you have the management leadership of the organization, it devolves on you to see that the parts relate to each other in a proper way. Misperceptions must be dispelled, and the staff must be made aware that the board has a specific role, too. You must make it clear that

1. As to that first "meddling" comment, the board has an accountability for monitoring all phases of the agency's functioning. This could involve inquiry as to details of staff activities to the point where it's interpreted by staff as meddling.

2. As to that "on high" comment, decisions that appear to be made in that manner are really the result of two dynamics. First, a board is frequently required to make the tough decisions that may be unpopular with one or another agency constituency, but consonant with the agency's overall interests. Second, those decisions are made after your own careful managerial (*staff*) study and recommendations.

Just as you, with the chair's support, must assure the board's respect of the staff, both professionally and personally, the converse must be the case as well. I'm not suggesting empty obsequiousness. I'm suggesting that you must call on your ingenuity to portray to staff enough of the information and background on a board's role so that there's a good understanding of how and why it acts. It won't be easy.

LESSON 46—THE GUNG-HO NEW BOARD CHAIR

It Can't Happen Here (You Wish!)

You've had it pretty easy up to now: a fairly effective board that meets quarterly and that accepts your recommendations with only a reasonable amount of interrogation and debate, and a chair who during his two-year tenure obediently stayed on his side of the leadership fence, but always responded to your requests for support and intervention when necessary. The agency hasn't been just drifting, of course, but you've been enjoying a pretty quiet professional environment. The annual meeting of the board was held last week and I was elected as the new chair. Things are about to change.

Let's see who the "I/me" is. I'm the dynamic president of the public utility serving the community. This is my second year on the board, and I've been openly critical of the "lack of dynamism" in the board's deliberations. (I've used that exact term at one of the board meetings.) I have now summoned (not invited) you to a breakfast meeting at my utility company office. Here's the dialogue.

Me: Welcome, Ms. X. I'm glad you were able to come on such short notice.

You (suppressing your real thoughts): Thanks for the invitation. Congratulations on your election to the chair. I certainly look forward to working with you during your tenure.

Me: That's why I asked you here—to tell you my ideas. I don't think my predecessor brought enough energy to the job. Most of our decisions were made after summary reports and recommendations from you—no offense intended, of course. There was very little lively discussion, and he ruled a few of my questions to you out of order. Things have to change now that I'm the chair. I consider myself personally accountable to the community for how this organization operates, just as if it were another public utility with me as its president. We're going to start to operate it just like a business (Oy Vey!—Lesson 17).

You: What specifics do you have in mind?

Me: I want to know every little detail of the agency's operations. That's the only way I can make the necessary changes. And I'm going to need a lot more information from you than I've been getting in the material that's sent out with the meeting agendas and your executive summary reports at the meetings. I have to know what's behind all of that.

You (noting the number of "I's" in that last outburst): I'll certainly help in any way I can.

Me: Good. Now here's the deal. You and I should meet here every Tuesday morning at 7. Bring with you the most current financial information and operational reports on our programs and services, as well as a schedule for me to meet with each staff member so that I can be familiar with what each does. I'll do those interviews at the agency's office.

You (in a wavering voice, but trying to be brave): Every Tuesday morning?

Me: No, not November 8, that's election day. So, can we get started next Tuesday?

You (shaken and wounded, but not fatally): Yes, of course. And thanks for the coffee.

Me: Just one more point before you go. At the last

meeting, there was discussion about our looking for a director of development. That should be easy; I've got just the person for the job.

You: Stage direction. Exit!

Okay, Just quiet down, 'ya hear? That's my advice. Take one full minute and inhale deeply five times. Then drive straight to the gym and get yourself up on that treadmill for a 40-minute workout. Then start reading the next paragraph.

Here's the deal. I remind you that up until now in this book, I've been coaching you on your responsibilities as the agency's management leader. Well, this scenario is going to call on every shred of your managerial skills. First of all, you're going to have to manage your own feelings of despair at the thought of having to deal with me on the terms that I've just announced. Look at it this way: I'm just another trustee who needs to be educated to his role. I may be a tougher case than some of the others, but that's really all it is—just another trustee to be educated. Then, when you've gotten yourself under control—and you simply *must*—you're going to have to get *me* under control by the principles of management that you know so well.

And here's a part of the concept of "management" that you may not know about and that I think will amuse you and make the challenge of taming me less redoubtable. (Sometimes it's helpful to go back into etymology.) The word "manage" evolves from vulgar (common, not academic) Latin, *manizare* and its particular root *manus*, meaning simple "hand." It evolved further into Italian and the word *maneggiare*, which meant "to handle, to take things in hand," but then began to take on the context of handling fractious or disobedient horses! Are you getting the picture? The actual word "manage" then came over into English around 1560, at which time it had the accepted meaning of training horses, and here we are.

Well, how are you going to train *me*? I have some suggestions, as follows:

1.   I assume you've quieted down. If not, keep trying 'til you do. Then, and only then, can you go on.

2.   Call *me* shortly after you quiet down and tell *me* how sincerely you welcome the opportunity of meeting with *me* on such a regular basis (try to *sound* sincere).

3.   Meet *me* that next Tuesday—and the next and the next and the next for several weeks—each time with volumes of financial and operational and programmatic information. Be prepared to be conversant on all of it. *Me*, as a "bottom-line" guy, I'll be saying "just the answers, ma'am," will soon see that *you* have everything under control, and I'll get a little bit tired of both that plethora of information that I've asked for and the early repetitious Tuesday morning meetings. You note that up to now, you haven't done anything about the other issues I've raised. But what you *have done is to have accomplished the most important first step—you have convinced **me** that **you** have administrative, managerial matters completely under control.* Now we're ready for the next phase of managing *me*.

4.   You now suggest to *me* two things: (a) that my time is too valuable to be spending on those same administrative, managerial matters that are already so clearly under your control, and (b) that you need *me* to weigh in on the bigger affairs and concerns of the agency, including corralling the rest of the trustees into the areas of legitimate governance concern where they can do the most good.

5.   And, "Oh yes," you go on to tell *me*, "if I as board chair interpose myself between you and

your staff people, I could easily undermine your position of authority as chief managerial officer without, of course, intending to do so."

6.   "And please, just one more thing," you tell *me*. "You may wish to announce at the next board meeting that if any trustee wants to submit to me a name for the possible position of director of development, he/she should feel free to do so. But please make them understand that I have the professional obligation of selecting subordinate staff and that I must do so without regard to the source of the name."

It may not all go exactly as planned, but it's better than abandoning ship. And I have the distinct feeling that *me* is now much more likely to be a better behaved horse.

LESSON 47—YOUR AGENCY CREATES A RELATED FOUNDATION

Are You Ready?

On this one, you can't just let matters happen. You have to take control if you want to retain your sanity (and, perhaps, your position).

You operate Safe House, a nonprofit agency providing services to victims of domestic violence. The idea emerges that the need for financial support is too great for your board to handle that issue in addition to the other affairs and concerns facing you. It's also acknowledged by your board itself, but somewhat grudgingly, that it doesn't have the "appropriate profile of members" (otherwise elsewhere known as the community elite) with access to their own wealth or the wealth of others. So the decision is made to create an institutionally related foundation. We're going to call Safe House the "host" agency and Safe House Foundation the "foundation."

Once created, this is a separate, freestanding legal entity with its own board (there may be some crossover of membership, but we'll note that later). And that board will have its own rights and accountabilities defined by its own governance documents. However, its sole mission is to raise, administer, and, eventually, transfer funds to the "host" agency to support its programs. Such relationships are often productive, sometimes troubled, and always complex. Some mutual dependence is necessary, but if the board of one party dominates the board of the other, or *intrudes on its proper role,* the result will be abject failure. Here is where the paid, professional leadership cohort— you—must take the reins in guiding the horses (remember Lesson 46?). The board will not know where to start. This gives you a hand in creating the environment in which you will be involved (embroiled?) during the rest of your tenure. Here are the hazards you'll encounter if the matter is not handled with your strong influence.

1. The foundation board will be dominated by too many host board members.

2. Host boards and foundation boards will sometimes dispute respective roles.

3. How well the host operates is, understandably, of concern to the foundation. (It's raising the money, remember!) Therefore, it may tend to meddle in the host's substantive affairs.

4. If that happens and the host responds impolitely, the foundation board will feel unappreciated. The reverse of this could also happen.

All of this requires, which I'm going to divide into two categories, "mindset rules" and "operational rules," both of which will require your intervention and approach (see Exhibit 9–1).

Exhibit 9–1 Rules for Trustees of the Host Agency and the Foundation Agency

---

For Host Trustees

Mindset rule

Recognize and respect the independence of the foundation and regard its trustees as equal-level colleagues, not subordinates.

Operational rules

1. Insist that the host board identify priority needs for financial support, and justify those needs in terms of the host's mission-related, goal-related, and program-related objectives.

2. Insist that the host's relationship with the foundation and the operating mechanisms between the two be clarified in writing—a statement of respective and collective roles and responsibilities, specifics such as employment of staff, budgetary support of staff, and policies for management of funds.

3. Establish a joint committee with foundation trustees to approve mutually agreed-on policies on fundraising, donor recognition, and so on, and to provide a forum for communication.

4. Provide opportunities for further, more informal, contacts with the foundation board.

5. To the extent possible, allow the foundation board to select its own members, with a minimum of cross-membership from the foundation board (one exception—see number 4 below).

For Foundation Trustees

Mindset rule

Recognize and accept the fact that your role is to raise and manage funds to meet the priority needs of the host as identified by the host's ED (you) and its board. Remember that gifts

---

(continues)

Exhibit 9–1 Continued

to the foundation are meant to benefit the host, not the foundation.

Operational rules

1. Insist on having the host's priorities identified, explained, and defended. You may "question" but not "fight for" priorities that you personally favor.

2. Establish written criteria for the selection of foundation trustees that reflect their responsibility to give, raise, and manage money.

3. Same as number 2 above.

4. Recognize the host's ED (you) as its leader and invite him/her to serve on the foundation board.

5. Provide opportunities for further, more informal, contacts with the host board.

LESSON 48—THE BOARD'S ACCOUNTABILITY FOR MANAGEMENT: A CONTRADICTION IN TERMS?

The "See to It That" Game

We have visited the issue so many times and we know the basics, all as set forth in Lesson 23.

- Me = governance, You = management

- Me = policy, You = administration

- Me = accountability, You = responsibility, duty and just for fun,

- Me = Tarzan, You = Jane (ask your parents about this one)

So, how do we have me accountable for management, which is clearly within your almost exclusive domain? Well, that's easy, and the term "almost exclusive" gives it away. If you go back to that lesson, it becomes pretty clear that my accountability as a board covers every aspect of the agency's functioning, *even your management function*. As far as the community is concerned, I'm accountable for you as well as for everything else that happens in the organization. Let's look more closely, however, at what that accountability entails. And here we go to another reference, Lesson 3, and particularly the first three areas of accountability specified there. These are the three that touch most directly on my accountability for you and for the management that you personify. Please note that each of these three is to be treated differently from all of the other areas of accountability devolving on me as your board. We refer to (a) selecting you as our ED, (b) supporting, advising, and encouraging you as our ED, and (c) assessing your performance as our ED.

As I emphasize to my class for aspiring EDs, the *duties* undergirding the actual functioning required by my other areas of accountability (i.e., fundraising, planning, furnishing facilities, and the like) are all in the category of the board "seeing to it that" it's done (we first used that phrase in Lesson 4. And I warned you that we'd be encountering it again). And, coincidentally, with further respect to these other areas of accountability, the board usually sees to its achievement by *seeing to it that **you** see to it that it's done*. And you probably see to it by assigning and allocating precise duties that bring about the fulfillment. Sometimes you use staff, sometimes volunteers, sometimes outside contractors, and sometimes board members themselves. In other words, as to these other areas, the duties themselves are delegable, so long as someone sees to it that they're performed.

But with respect to the three that involve you, the board doesn't just see to it that, it *performs* them.

Here's the theory.

The board is, indeed, so inextricably accountable for the quality and the parameters and the intensely close personal nature of its relationship with you, the ED, that the very duties undergirding these three are to be performed by the board itself. They are not delegable. "Seeing to it that" in this context, means doing it oneself/themselves.

As to the first, selecting the ED, I must admit that in modern times, the board may want to involve the services of a professional headhunter. If so, I recommend that its role be, at most, to help the board in composing the advertising for the national search (if there is one) and perhaps in thinning down the field of candidates who emerge. However, the duties, or you may call them responsibilities, if you wish, of deciding on the professional and personal qualities of the person being sought, as well as taking the ultimate act of selection, devolve solely on the board.

The same is true of the second area of the board's accountability: supporting, advising, and encouraging you. The board is the group that has the insights and that knows most intimately the professional issues that you encounter on behalf of the agency. I refer to problems with staff or with programs or with the community or the funders, for example, or with the whirlwind of conflicting expectations that are heaped on you by our various and diverse constituencies. It knows, therefore, when the support button or the advice button or the encouragement button should be pushed. As to personal issues, again, it has the insights to know when you're plagued by problems of personal health or compensation equity or family dislocations. And here again, it's called on to push the right button. These are acts that must be performed directly by the trustees and cannot, in fairness to you, be delegated to any other.

As to the third accountability, assessing your performance, we've already suggested (Lesson 31) mechanisms and criteria for doing so. We emphasize here, however, only that this too is non-delegatable by the board. Clearly, they're the best judges of your leadership achievements and style. With them, you're always "on stage."

LESSON 49—*YOUR* ACCOUNTABILITY FOR MANAGEMENT

It's a "Coping" Thing

Throughout the previous lessons, I've referred to your role as manager of the agency or, more officially, as ED. Elsewhere in the nonprofit literature, you might be referred to as the chief executive officer or the president, or some other such impressive or intimidating title. In any of such instances, we envision an office that has the necessary "immediate authority" to ensure that the agency operates in an orderly, efficient, and effective manner in all of its functions—no small task. If at the outset you are the only staff person, then you occupy, *ex officio,* the position of director of everything—of development, of programs, of volunteers, and so on. I've seen many of you in that situation, and you usually complain bitterly about the weight of the responsibility. You wish you had some help there at the top, at least a director of budgeting, you tell me (I'm your chair, remember). However, that may be an unwise wish, the fulfillment of which may be to your still further annoyance. Strange as it may seem, in your position as sole staff member, your job is really relatively easy, relatively simple, compared to what it becomes as soon as your first staff person comes aboard. For then you become, more specifically now, not only your own director of development, of programs, and of volunteers, as before, but, with the addition of your new person, you become the director of human resources as well. The addition has two immediate ramifications. First, whereas previously you had the accountability only for your own actions, duties, and responsibilities, you now have the accountability for *her* actions, duties, and responsibilities as well. Second, there is an additional *range and category* of actions, duties, and responsibilities devolving on you. The very staff that you wished for now becomes another component of agency functioning for you to *manage.* This, in turn, means creating, implementing, and enforcing staff-level policies for:

- hiring
- discharge
- job descriptions
- delegation of duties
- evaluation
- compensation and rewarding
- the full range of personnel rules and practices
- re-setting internal goals

Please note this carefully: *Your responsibilities, your areas of accountability, never lessen with the addition of staff; they increase.* And let's make that point even more clearly: When in the course of events you have a sufficient number of staff people to warrant the employment of a separate director of human resources, the dance goes on. And when *she* starts actually functioning as your director of human resources, you're going to have to "see to it that" she does her job in a commendable manner. Get the point? (At the end of this lesson, I'm going to elaborate on the "see to it that" game.)

So the burdens of management just seem to pile on. How do we "manage" those burdens of management, which become, then, another dimension of management itself? That requires some analysis.

My own experience in life is that there's a first and foremost condition precedent for being able to manage; that is, *being able to cope! Life as an ED is not for cowards or sissies.* And "to cope" implies a mindset that has its origin in the Romantic Languages.

In French ("coup"), it refers to "the striking of a blow." In Latin ("colaphus"), it becomes more specific, "a blow with the fist." Both seem to imply defiance, but that's not the point I want to make. It's more the matter of courage and the facing of reality than it is of defiance. Let's just say it's *semi-defiance*. One of the definitions in Webster's *Third New International Dictionary* fits this lesson just fine. The definition has two parts: (a) to face or encounter a problem, and (b) to find necessary expedients to overcome it. The first is the "coping" part, and you know what that means from the above definition. The second is the "managing" part, which is also defined.[1]

There will be times during your tenure when the problems before you will range from the seemingly insurmountable, such as an out-of-control board, a financial scandal, a programmatic scandal, or an ethical scandal, to a mere toe-stubber, such as a renegade employee or an interpersonal dispute between staff or a non-functioning computer or heating system. If serious enough, the world will seem out of joint. What do you do? The answer is the two-step response we've noted above. First, you'll cope; second, you'll manage. First, you'll set your jaw in semi-defiance and stand fully resolved to meet the challenge of the particular problem. And then, but only then, you'll engage that huge creative brain of yours in how to find necessary expedients to overcome it.

In a way, I suppose, trying to be a successful ED who responds rationally and effectively to your ever-increasing, ever more complicated problems is like a version of "Mission Impossible." But, just remember, you are a specialist in coping. And once you have the problem isolated by coping with it, I know you can do it.

Now a bit about the "see to it that" game, as promised.

1.   It starts with the board's role—the ultimate authority, you'll remember. That role requires that the

---

[1] *Webster's Third New International Dictionary, Unabridged* (G. and C. Merriam Co. 1971.)

board, in its monitoring capacity—and being just a bunch of lay persons—*see to it that* all of the agency's functions are being carried out in a commendable way. How does it perform that rather overwhelming role?

2.   It engages *you* to *see to it that* you *see to it that* all of the agency's functions are being carried out in a commendable way. How do *you* do that?

3.   *You* engage staff to *see to it that they see to it that* each such staff person involved in any of the agency's functions is carrying it out in a commendable way.

So there you are—right in the middle of the board and the staff in this *see to it that* thing. But it gets even more complicated. Because, as we've stated in Lesson 6, we have this other irony to deal with: Because you are the prime educator to you board, because the board will be looking to you for what it should do and know, it may not be aware of the reality that it must (a) *see to it that* (b) *you* *see to it that* (c) *staff sees to it that* all of this falls into place. So be sure that you use this "see to it that" game as an educational tool for your board.

LESSON 50—LIVING WITH RISKS

It Happens in the Nonprofit World, Too

You've worked all these years as ED of a home for runaway girls who have been victimized by domestic violence. It's been a blessing to the community and to the scores of young women who now live their lives in relative security. You have an effective and supportive board, a cooperative staff, a corps of reliable volunteers, and a fine facility for referral services and first echelon care. Yet there are hazards that could threaten it all—loss to property caused by outside factors (fire, flood, lightning, collision), and loss caused by inside factors (wrongful acts by someone affiliated with the organization).

Your first thought is to acquire insurance for the purpose of shifting the loss. That's a good thought to pursue, and here's my advice to you as you pursue it: Engage the best professional person available to you whose area of concentration is to advise on and furnish the right kind of insurance protection. It should of course include protection against damage to the agency's property, as well as exposure to claims against the agency for its activities and alleged wrongdoing of the agency itself and those affiliated with it. Your professional person may be a lawyer or an insurance agent or both. In discussing the recommended protection, be sure to consider

1.   the premium cost

2.   the policy limits on coverage:

   • per incident of damage loss or claim

   • the total of such losses and claims during the policy term

3.   the "deductible"—the amount of loss or claim for which the agency must retain responsibility

4.   the "affiliate" coverage on claims (i.e., coverage for trustees, staff, volunteers, etc.)

5.   types of claims covered (definition of "wrongful acts")

6.   exclusions: types of claims not covered

7.   defense expense issues (This is particularly important, because legal expense in defending claims for wrongdoing represents a big possible exposure.)

   • coverage for the "first dollar" of expense

   • coverage for the defense even of excluded claims

- advancement of expenses of defense (whose responsibility?)

I mention all of these not to have you substitute your judgment for that of the professionals, but only so you can discuss these provisions not only with your professionals, but also with your trustees. Each may be a variable with respect to the premium, and this should be in your mind.

Obviously, we have been dealing with *shifting* potential loss or exposure. But I'm certain that you're going to convince your board that this does not preclude your trying to *avoid* potential loss or exposure. And for this, there's no substitute for careful, prudent, and responsible functioning. Although I hate to sound like a cynic, here's a checklist to begin with.

- Avoid "too much trust" in key personnel for "too long."

- Avoid poor financial recordkeeping.

- Be aware of, and in compliance with, applicable laws on employee rights, discrimination, and other human resource issues.

- Compile clear practices for hiring, including the conducting of background reviews.

- Compile clear policies against conflict of interest.

- Compile clear policies as to "off-duty" conduct.

LESSON 51—"HUMANE, COMPASSIONATE, AND BENEVOLENT" REVISITED

Emperor Asoka, Where Are You Now?

In my role as a sentimental old fool, I have the tendency to return frequently to the question of what constitutes the soul of the nonprofit world. And I conclude now, as I have occasionally throughout this text, that it is made up of a decision on the part of some person or agency to offer help to someone else in need—any act large or small—to reduce that someone else's burden. And there's an additional necessary element—that the offeror does so with no thought of self-interest. The offeror need not be the Red Cross or an agency of equivalent size; it can be a simple human who decides to reach out to another human. It involves the offer of human, compassionate, and benevolent service; the offeror represents the soul of what this book is all about. In closing, then, I want to tell you about a cluster of events in the life of my family and me that illustrate my point.

Just about halfway through my career as a lawyer—the 23rd year of my 46-year stint with my firm—I took a self-imposed one-year sabbatical. My partners were shocked: How could I afford a year of corporate lawyer-level income? I had no answer to that. I probably couldn't, but I was going to anyway. Their spouses were shocked even more. If Lewis can do it, dammit Harold, why can't you? Or why can't we ever get away even for a weekend? Or at the very least, why can't you come home for dinner on time once in a while?

Our friends were shocked, too. A fishing village on the north coast of Crete? (Yes.) Won't the kids miss a year of school? (Yes, they will.) What if you get sick? (We'll try to avoid it.) What about the language? (We speak enough Greek to get along.) Where will you live? (We've arranged for a little house with a terrace overlooking the Gulf of Mirabello, part of the beautiful Aegean.) What about getting around? (We've bought a donkey. Her name's Eleni—Helen—and her face would surely launch a thousand ships.) There were other questions, and we were able to answer all of them to *our* satisfaction, if not to the satisfaction of the questioners.

You see, they all missed the point. They should have known just from being our friends and being aware of the circumstances of our lives. My wife Joanne, who had never been married before, had the courage to marry into a household with three ready-made sons—I had been a widower. Within a little more than two years, our family included two daughters 11 months apart. There was much to be done within the family by way of integrating the diverse lives of five children and two parents. Each day had a crisis or two that was not easily or fully addressed when the parents had to answer to the demanding professional responsibilities of being a lawyer (me) or a writer and historian (Joanne). We found that at the end of the day, Joanne and I were giving each other what was left of each other—not fair to either of us or the kids. So we decided to disengage. The two older boys were already in graduate schools, en route to their careers in education and medicine. So Joanne and David and little Pavia (named after a beautiful medieval city in northern Italy) and Clea (named after a remote archaeological site in southern Sicily) and I boarded the Cristoforo Columbo in New York and sailed away to Piraeus, the port of Athens, and then on to the village of Aghios Nikolaos (Saint Nicholas) in Crete.

What has all of this to do with the nonprofit world? It gave me a chance to verify the type of human conduct that personifies its soul, without requiring a formalized agency or mechanism. I've already used Uncle Louie and Tommy Christmas as examples. Well, we found the whole island of Crete to be an informal version of a more well-known "official" nonprofit agency: The Travelers' Aid Society. Wherever we turned, we were accorded acts of kindness. And I began to realize that those acts of kindness had their basis in the Greek language itself.

It starts with the Greek word "xenos"—this is the anglicized version. That word, in modern Greek, simply means "stranger." It is the root word for xenophobia, meaning fear of the stranger or of the alien or of even the poor immigrant. Yet in ancient Greek, the root word had the context of a "sacred person." Here's why. In antiquity, travel was a hard challenge; villages only a kilometer apart, as the crow flies, could be days apart on foot. And the journey had to be made over roadless expanses, through forests and across hills and streams and under danger from bears and mountain lions. If, notwithstanding those treacherous challenges, a stranger, a xenos, appeared in your village, it could very well be Apollo or Zeus in disguise, testing your sense of kindness. So you damn well better treat him with the utmost courtesy and respect.

You see, to the ancients of that civilization, there were only three unforgivable sins: blasphemy against the gods, the shedding of kindred blood (killing a spouse was not "kindred blood"), and, believe it or not, this was the equivalent of the first two, mistreatment of a host or guest! So we, as strangers (xenoi) in the villages of the island of Crete, were the beneficiaries of scores of acts of kindness. It was nice to be mistaken for an Olympian god. But it got to this point: If we were in a remote area looking for a long abandoned archaeological site or a hidden cave or cove, we learned *not* to ask the nearby shepherd for directions. Because if we did, he'd insist on climbing into our jeep and guiding us there, leaving his dogs in charge of the flock. And once we arrived at our destination, he would then insist on *walking* back to his sheep so as not to inconvenience us. If we had driven him back, his act would not have qualified in his mind as an act of kindness. So he just left us "meh ta podia," with his own two feet.

When a stranger is in need of help, we learned, he can be sure that the Greek who offers it will also offer a lasting friendship. Joanne and I and David and the two little girls arrived at the Heraklion, Crete airport late one night on our return journey home from a sojourn in Turkey. The girls were tired and cranky and we decided to stay at a hotel in that town until the next day, when we'd make the 90 kilometer return trip to Aghios Nikolaos. I engaged a taxi and asked the driver, Eleutherios Stratigakis, whom we had never met before, to wait until we claimed our luggage. But it soon appeared that there was the not-unusual complication for Olympic Airways—our luggage did not arrive; it was lost somewhere. Seeing the children restless and weary, Eleutherios Stratigakis ("soldier of freedom") herded us all gently into his taxi. When I asked him, "What about the luggage?" he made the grand gesture of a Cretan. This involves snapping the heels together sharply, closing the eyes, raising oneself to one's full height, jutting the chin out, and bringing the right arm up and around in a full half-circle as if to begin an exaggerated salute, but then bending the arm at the elbow so that the hand finally rests flat on the breast. That very complex gesture has a very simple meaning: It means that he, the gesturer, assures you that the problem will be solved and that he will solve it.

So, quietly and obediently, we were driven to the nearby hotel and dropped there for the night. And by the next morning, our bags had been retrieved and delivered by Eleutherios and he left his telephone number where we could call him to arrange our trip back to our village. But this was only the beginning. It developed that his father was a vintner who produced, he claimed, the best wine on the island. And so we can testify, because a few days later, Eleutherios came all the way out to our village to deliver to us a gift from his father—a cask of his best wine. And thereafter, from time to time, whenever Eleutherios had a "tourist run" in our vicinity of the island, he would bring out more jugs of wine to fill our casks. That's the kind of neighborliness we yearn for in everyday life, isn't it? Too bad that these days, it has to come almost exclusively from incorporated nonprofits.

Perhaps the most startling and welcome act of kindly intervention occurred late one December afternoon. And I could have sworn that it came directly from the heavenly heavens, from an Olympic deity. We were hosting a visit from friends from Westchester County, a physician (Lowell) and his teacher wife (Susan). As a special adventure, we had decided to take them to a remote Minoan archaeological site called Vathypetro, in the center of the island. We had not been there before, and our crude map only hinted at its exact position. We drove to a nearby village and stopped too long at the village cafe—it was growing later and later and darker and darker—to converse with the villagers. When we asked directions to Vathypetro, several of the villagers offered to ride with us, but there was no room in our little car. We left them with their enjoinder to us that the road to Vathypetro was "kakos," meaning bad. That description was an understatement. It was also a surprise to hear it. Most Greeks optimistically describe even the word road as "kalos," or good, no matter how bad it is.

As we left the village, the road deteriorated into a double mule track, just wide enough to accommodate the wheels of our car. There were thick, unbroken hedgerows on both sides, so there was no way of turning around. After a few kilometers of increasing uncertainty, we came to a fork. I was in despair as to which way to go. I stopped. I saw a pole sticking up out of the ground and I saw that a sign that it once held had fallen to the ground. I picked up the sign and it read "Vathpetro," but there was no directional arrow. Lowell detected my nervousness, and in a tone of half derision, half fright, asked me what I intended to do *now*. In a show of baseless bravado, I told him that I was to revert to doing what the ancients did when they were facing a dilemma.

"What is exactly that?" he asked.

"I'm going to appeal to the gods," I answered.

And with that, I cupped my hands over my mouth and shouted toward the heavens in my best ancient Greek: "Great gods, when I get back to Aghios Nikolaos, I shall sacrifice to you a lamb and a chicken. Please favor us: What is the direction to Vathypetro?"

There was silence, except for the echo of my voice coming back from the high surrounding hills. Lowell asked me what I had shouted, and he muttered "ridiculous." But then, suddenly, there came an answer. A mysterious, melodious voice from above announced "Aristera! Aristera!" which means "To the left! To the left!"

Lowell turned ashen white as, in triumph, I curtly told him to get back in the car so we could continue our journey. As I was about to climb back into the driver's seat, I saw the figure of a shepherd on the crest of a nearby hill. He had been watching our movements and simply shouted down an answer to my plea for directions. I never disclosed that to Lowell.

Ten Questions for Every Trustee

I t's hardly likely that any would-be trustee is going to be recruited with such a direct, candid, and demanding approach, and I suppose that we have to face that reality. Before-the-fact demands could, I admit, be quite discouraging to someone whom we really want to attract to the board, so I'll give a little on this. Maybe just some generalities will do, just so long as he or she isn't encouraged to believe that it's just a dilletantish dalliance. But there's a big "however" here. Somewhere along the line, every trustee *must be made aware of* what's expected, and the sooner the better. And if the message can't be effectively delivered by lecturing on the material in Tom Ingram's book, there's an alternative. Three other people at the National Center for Nonprofit Boards (NCNB, Sandra Hughes, Berit Lakey, and Marla Bobowick) have compiled a neat little list of 10 questions that you and your board chair can present to each trustee at some appropriate time. It's part of NCNB's *The Board Building Cycle,* and each question clearly implies one part of what the

Source: Reprinted with permission from R.T. Ingram, *Ten Basic Responsibilities of Nonprofit Boards* © 1996, National Center for Nonprofit Boards.

trustee should be knowing or doing. Also, each clearly implies that my performance is directly related to how well *you* are comporting with Lesson 6, in which you are identified as the chief educator to your board. It's a matter of pride for you if I answer all of those questions in the affirmative. Here they are:

1. Do I understand and support the mission of the organization?

Clearly, the reasons for someone to serve on the board of an organization are belief in its mission and the intention to support its mission enthusiastically. Any other reason has to be either irrelevant or a basis for suspicion (e.g., personal or professional networking, visibility in the community, another line in one's curriculum vitae). Personally, I can't think of another *good* reason. You know that after 46 years as a lawyer and a career on behalf of hundreds of clients, I have only one client left, and that's the concept of trusteeship. Therefore, my own rule for board membership is a strict one: I declare that when one pledges to be a member of a board, he/she agrees to dedicate his/her entire sphere of influence to help further the agency's mission. (It follows, by the way, that if one is expected to dedicate his/her "entire sphere of influence," and because there is, by definition, only one "entire sphere of influence," then serving on more than one nonprofit board at any one time is a clear conflict of interest. You should know that when I promote this idea before some of my consultancy audiences, I sometimes get booed off the stage. Earlier in this book, you'll find other so-called Lewis Rules that are equally unpopular.)

2. Am I knowledgeable about the organization's programs and services?

How can I *not* be, and still be an effective trustee? If, indeed, I have the ultimate authority and accountability for all that happens in the agency, it's not a big step to conclude that I really ought to know about how it functions in the delivery of the programmatic services that support its mission and goals—what's being done and at what level of quality. In this book, I try to emphasize that the board's level of concern should be focused mainly on mission-related and goal-related issues (governance) and much less formally on program-related issues (management). I do so partly in defense of you, my ED, and your turf, and to discourage too much board meddling. But here again, *you must do your part in avoiding my purported acts of meddling by keeping me so comfortably informed about details of agency functioning—its programs and services— that I don't feel the need to meddle!*

3. Do I follow trends and important developments related to this organization?

The answer to this may depend on how well you follow the precepts in Lessons 7 and 8, *infra*. In those lessons, we have noted, in greater detail than we do here, that (a) the board's ownership of its own functioning requires that it have a mechanism for continuing education of trustees (Lesson 7), and that (b) this includes five areas of knowledge, one of them being trends in the delivery of like services by like agencies, and the other being trends in society (Lesson 8). We've made it clear that all of that requires both ED leadership and support. So if I answer "no" to this, you *and* I (your board chair) had better look at each other squarely in the eye and shamefully point fingers.

4. Do I assist with fundraising and/or give a significant annual gift to the organization?

Here again, I refer you to one of our lessons, Lesson 12, the "resources" lesson. If you and I have done our jobs, there is no question that by now I have a full understanding of what's expected of me. Now the only question is whether or not I'm fulfilling the expectation.

5. Do I read and understand the organization's financial statements?

Two parts to this question, Ms. ED—the meaningful part is "understand." So let's get to that. Nobody's born with a natural fascination for balance sheets and operating (profit/loss in the for-profit world) statements. In fact, most of us have a feeling for them that is somewhere between anathema and disinterest. I personally take the position that if trustees start analyzing line items in budgets and financial statements, they're either (a) focusing at the wrong level of their responsibilities, or (b) showing off. But I'm in the distinct minority. So if any of your trustees answers "no," you know exactly what to do: Identify the liveliest teacher of accounting that you can find and hire him or her for a one and one-half hour class on reading financial statements (two hours is too long—everyone will fall asleep) as a required-attendance mini-retreat.

6. Do I have a good working relationship with the chief executive (you)?

There's a frivolous approach to that. It could be said that if I don't, it's because you haven't read this book and applied its various lessons for how to instruct me, educate me, massage me, exploit me, use the board chair to discipline me and keep me at the right level of inquiry—I could go on. But the less frivolous approach is to make sure there's an *environment* in the organization that allows me to have that good working relationship. Your endless list of responsibilities includes establishing, and then nurturing, that ephemeral status called our "working relationship." This includes, I must remind you, not only all of the mechanisms referred to above as "frivolous" (they're not), but also your personal skills in building the professional part of our working relationship *and* the personal part. As examples of the professional building part, draw me out on why I'm on the board and on what committee(s) I can best serve (this is for consultation with your board chair), and ask me to be constructively critical of whatever I've observed during my tenure. As to the personal building part, invite yourself to lunch with me, give me a personal tour of the facilities, and call me for an occasional bit of advice when my work/life/interests coincide with an issue confronting the agency and when you sincerely want my help.

That all takes time, doesn't it? But when I answer this sixth question, it'll be all in your favor.

7. Do I recommend individuals for service to this board?

See Lesson 7 on this issue. If you've done a good job of demanding that the board accept the incidents of agency ownership therein referred to, then it's a snap. Look at Mechanism I, the recruitment mechanism. If your board governance committee, or whatever you call it, has developed this mechanism, then most clearly it will have required my recommendation of individuals for board service. Too bad, of course, that this too depends on your initiative, but that's the way it is.

8. Do I prepare for and participate in board meetings and committee meetings?

Let's answer a question with a question: Where do *you* fit in on this? It would be nice if you didn't have to, but you do. The primary responsibility for getting me to answer "yes" on this devolves clearly on the shoulders of the board chair, not you—he's the disciplinarian on these matters. He's the one who must insist that every trustee read, study, and understand all the material that is sent out in respect of a board or committee meeting. He's the one who must make committee assignments of personnel and issues. He's the one who must enforce board and committee attendance requirements. Right? Right! But now it's time for the ever-popular "however." However, dammit, he may just not know or remember all of that *unless you take it upon yourself to remind him!*

9. **Do I act as a goodwill ambassador to the organization?**

This is easy. All I have to say about this is in Lesson 13. But remember, it's another "see to it that" situation in which you're the see to it that gal (or guy).

10. **Do I find serving on the board to be a satisfying and rewarding experience?**

If you're responsible for a "yes" answer here, I have another question for you: Do you still want to be an ED?

Tax Compliance Issues: A Primer for Nonprofit Executive Directors

imply stated, the Internal Revenue Service (IRS) salutes your agency's nonprofit status by exempting you from taxes on the income that it earns from its nonprofit services. Why? Because it's assumed that you're making some contribution to the welfare of some segment of society—thereby assisting the government in the performance of its functioning. And, if you achieve the more exalted status of a 501 (c) (3) organization, the IRS allows the taxpayer who contributes to your agency to deduct from his or her otherwise-taxable income some amount of that contribution.

But as is usually the case with something that is "simply stated," it's just not that simple.

No matter what size your nonprofit is, your organization is going to need an accountant. You don't necessarily need to have an accountant on staff; most major accounting firms have specialists in nonprofit financial management on staff, and

Source: Reprinted from A. Dzamba, *The Nonprofit Executive's Tax Desk Annual,* © 2001, Aspen Publishers, Inc.

many smaller firms specialize in nonprofit accounting. Take care of that issue the morning of your first day on the job.

Still, it is important for every ED to have a general knowledge of nonprofit tax issues. Ignorance of the law is not an excuse that is looked on favorably by the IRS. Although some top managers have used ignorance as a defense, many of these are now *former* EDs.

What follows is a brief look at tax considerations for nonprofit organizations.

TYPES OF NONPROFIT ORGANIZATIONS

Congress has provided a number of different classifications for nonprofit organizations. For the most part, these organizations are defined in IRS Code Section 501 (c). This is why you have probably heard the term 501 (c)(3) used as a synonym for nonprofit. In fact, there are more than 20 different classifications under the IRS code, but most nonprofits fall into one of the following types:

- 501 (c) (3): organizations operated for religious, charitable, scientific, literary, or educational purposes; testing for public safety; fostering national or international sports competitions; or the prevention of cruelty to children or animals

- 501 (c) (4): civic leagues, social welfare organizations, or local associations of employees

- 501 (c) (5): labor, agricultural, or horticultural organizations

- 501 (c) (6): business leagues, chambers of commerce, real estate boards, boards of trade, or professional football leagues

There are well over one million nonprofits that exist in the United States, not including churches, which are not required to report to the IRS.

OBTAINING AND MAINTAINING TAX-EXEMPT STATUS

Nonprofits receive favorable attention from the IRS because they are not operated for the purposes of making a profit. But, it's somewhat more complicated than that.

For example, a 501 (c) (3) must be organized and operated exclusively for a religious, charitable, scientific, literary, educational, test for the public safety, prevention of cruelty to children or animals, or promotion of amateur sports competition. No part of the organization's net earnings may benefit any individual or private shareholder. In addition, the organization may not devote a substantial part of its activities to attempting to influence legislation. Moreover, the organization may not participate or intervene in any political campaign on behalf of (or in opposition to) any candidate for public office.

The IRS is responsible for granting tax-exempt status to nonprofits. Organizations that wish to qualify under Section 501 (c) (3) must file Form 1023, "Application for Recognition of Exemption under Section 501 (c) (3)," with the IRS. Other organizations are required to file Form 1024, "Application for Recognition of Exemption Under 501 (a)." Forms must be filed with the IRS district director for the area where the organization's primary office is located. Organizations must file these applications within 15 months after the close of the month in which the organization first came into existence, in order to qualify for tax-exempt status as of that date.

That sounds simple, but the reality is that these forms are difficult to complete. Organizations interested in obtaining nonprofit status must provide a large amount of information, such as statements of revenue and expenses for the current year and up to three prior years. New organizations are required to supply proposed budgets for the next two years.

And it is more than just Forms 1023 or 1024. Each application requires an application fee, the amount of which is based on the size of your budget; Form 8718 ("User Fee for Exempt Organization Determination Letter Request"); a copy of the organization's articles of incorporation; a copy of the organization's bylaws; and Form SS-4, which is the application for an employer identification number (EIN), unless a number has already been received.

After the IRS receives this package of materials, it issues a "determination letter." A favorable determination letter grants tax-exempt status. If that isn't granted, the IRS will send out a "proposed adverse determination letter," which an organization may appeal to the IRS national office. Nonprofits looking for 501 (c) (3) status ordinarily receive an advance ruling letter, which provides a provisional period—usually five years—during which the organization is assumed to meet the public charity requirements. Within 90 days after the end of the provisional period, the organization must submit some additional information to prove its compliance with the IRS requirements, and the IRS will issue a determination letter.

IRS officials can, and sometimes do, revoke an organization's tax-exempt status. To maintain your organization's exemption, your nonprofit must continue to operate under the prescribed IRS guidelines. The IRS also requires most organizations to file the following annual information returns:

- Form 990, "Return of Organization Exempt from Income Tax," for all nonprofits (except those required to file Form 990-PF, or those that qualify to file form 990-EZ)

- Form 990-PF, "Return of Private Foundation," for 501 (c) (3) organizations that do not qualify as public charities

- Form 990-EZ, "Short Form Return of Organizations Exempt from Income Tax," for tax-exempt organizations with gross receipts of less than $100,000 and total assets of less than $250,000 at the end of the year

- Schedule A, an attachment to Form 990 for section 501 (c) (3) nonprofits that file either Form 990 or Form 990-EZ

Although the IRS code includes a variety of special rules and exemptions regarding public charity status, most 501 (c) (3) organizations obtain and maintain their status by continuing to meet the "public support test." This requires that a public charity receive at least one-third of its total revenue from the general public. This support includes direct donations, indirect contributions, and funds through government units. If an organization receives its funding through another nonprofit, these amounts will normally count as indirect contributions from the general public.

Amounts that *do not* count as public support include investment income, receipts from trade or business activities, and contributions from single donors, to the extent they exceed 2 percent of the organization's total support. To determine the public support number, an organization normally reviews the four years immediately preceding the current year so as to arrive at whether the test is met.

Although a nonprofit receiving tax-exempt status does not have to pay income taxes, it still must pay federal employment taxes (FICA), state unemployment taxes, and federal and state excise taxes. Some nonprofits must also pay federal unemployment taxes and, in some states, sales and use taxes. This is another area where the help of an accountant is often necessary.

Be especially careful when considering your payroll taxes. In recent years, the IRS has cracked down on the subject of independent contractors, looking at whether or not these individuals are actually employees. Some nonprofits have ended up with rather large tax bills following an IRS audit.

WHEN A NONPROFIT RECEIVES BUSINESS INCOME

The unrelated business income tax (UBIT) can cast a shadowy figure over a nonprofit's entrepreneurial ideas. Accountants say that every year, more nonprofits become subject to UBIT. This stems from two primary factors.

- Nonprofits are finding it more difficult to raise the necessary funds through traditional means, and are turning to money-making ideas that draw the attention of the IRS.

- Each tax season, the IRS seems to become more adept at identifying and collecting UBIT.

If a nonprofit organization engages in a business that is "unrelated" to its exempt purpose, thus competing with for-profits in that particular business, IRS officials believe that the organization should pay taxes on that income. Sounds simple, but the theory has led to complex rules.

It makes sense for many nonprofits to enter into nontraditional fundraising—and many boards push for new fundraising rather than raising fees or membership dues. But before doing so, it would be wise for an organization to develop a solid understanding of the rules and analyze the costs and benefits of any new activity. When an ED gets into trouble with her board, finances are often the reason.

TEN TIPS TO AVOID COMMON TAX ERRORS

Because the tax laws are so mind-boggling, all nonprofits make mistakes. The trick is to understand the most common tax-related errors that nonprofit managers unwittingly make. Not only can some of these blunders cost your nonprofit financial penalties, but they may even result in its nonprofit status being revoked. Here are 10 tips that will help prevent these inadvertent foul-ups.

1. Report changes in activities to the IRS. Your nonprofit has a continuing obligation to inform the IRS of significant changes in its character, purpose, or methods of operation. For example, adding or dis-

continuing a program or publication would be a reportable change.

What to do: Use your annual IRS return to review the year's activities and to determine if there have been any changes you need to report. You must explain any changes in an attachment to your return.

2. Don't overlook IRS conditions in ruling letters. A nonprofit's original tax-exemption letter from the IRS often contains special conditions for maintaining exempt status.

What to do: Make sure your organization is complying with the terms of its original exemption letter. Otherwise, your nonprofit's exempt status could be revoked—retroactively.

3. Analyze every income-producing activity. As noted earlier, the IRS has a long history of cracking down on UBIT, which is money derived from commercial activities that are not connected to a nonprofit's tax-exempt mission.

What to do: Scrutinize each of your nonprofit's income-producing activities to determine the correct treatment for UBIT purposes.

4. Watch expense allocations. Keep careful records of staff and expenses associated with particular activities. For example, staff members should be filling out daily time cards detailing the time spent between, for example, fundraising and general management duties.

What to do: Make sure your nonprofit is using a reasonable method for allocating expenses between activities—and put it in writing. For example, allocating salaries and benefits expenses based on time spent would be reasonable.

5. Document transactions with related entities. Make sure any transactions with other exempt organiza-

tions, such as expense-sharing arrangements and loans, are carefully documented. The IRS wants to be assured that your nonprofit's assets aren't being diverted from its exempt purposes.

What to do: Any loans should be on an arm's length basis and should be documented with a loan agreement. Also, note the loan transaction in board minutes.

6. File complete, accurate IRS returns. More than half of nonprofit IRS returns contain material errors. Surprisingly, this includes returns prepared by professional accountants.

What to do: Make sure there's enough time allotted to complete—and for you to review—the returns.

7. Maintain adequate books and records. The IRS is not only concerned with your organization's financial records.

What to do: Make sure your nonprofit's corporate minute book is updated with minutes from all board meetings and executive committee meetings. All amendments to your non-profit's governing documents, such as the articles of incorporation and bylaws, must be included in the minutes.

8. Don't misclassify employees as independent contractors. Nonprofit employers that misclassify employees as independent contractors are liable for back payroll taxes and penalties. Generally, the question of worker classifications is resolved by applying a 20-factor common law test.

What to do: Make sure all independent contractor arrangements are in writing and are reviewed by a professional adviser who is thoroughly familiar with the distinctions.

9. Observe lobbying rules. Nonprofits are subject to restrictions on lobbying activities. For example, a charity that claims exemption under Section 501 (c) (3) will lose its exempt status if it engages in "sub-

stantial" lobbying activities. However, what constitutes "substantial" lobbying isn't spelled out in the tax law or regulations.

What to do: The IRS urges charities to make the formal lobbying election under Section 501 (h) of the Internal Revenue Code. It sets allowable dollar limits on lobbying expenditures.

10. Comply with public inspection rules. Your nonprofit must make available for public inspection (a) its annual IRS return and (b) its original approved application to the IRS for tax exemption. These items must be made available during regular business hours at your organization's principal office and at any satellite office having three or more employees. Your annual IRS return (e.g., Form 990) must be available for three years, beginning with its due date. The only part of the form you can withhold from public inspection is the list of your nonprofit's substantial contributors.

What to do: Review your public inspection policies and procedures. Make sure they comply with recently enacted rules that require you to also provide copies of these documents to anyone who requests them.

Accounting Issues: A Primer for Nonprofit Executive Directors

I f you ever invite me to a board of trustees session on "How to Read a Financial Statement," I'll either just turn you down or ask for your expulsion. My attitude is fixed: I don't have to know about that stuff as long as you do. So that makes the matter quite clear: You do "have to know about that stuff." And, in fairness to you, if you need such a session (or a lot of sessions) on the subject, I'll see to it that the board provides you with the opportunity. Some knowledge of accounting is a must.

A few nonprofit executives come into the job with at least some background in accounting. If you are not among them, take some time to understand accounting basics before you go too far.

For some, this basic look at accounting will seem rather elementary. But for other new EDs, it may serve as a warning that they are leading more than just a cause: They are leading

Source: Reprinted from A.S. Lang, *Practical Guide in Nonprofit Financial Management,* © 1995, Aspen Publishers, Inc.

an operation with many of the same questions and problems that face their for-profit colleagues.

BASIC ACCOUNTING CONCEPTS

Accountants work with five broad categories when reporting to an organization's financial activity. These categories are assets, liabilities, equity, revenue, and expense. These terms may be familiar; like many accounting and financial terms, they are part of everyday life.

Assets, Liabilities, and Equity

Consider the first two of these categories, assets and liabilities, the accounting terms that describe "what you own" and "what you owe." *Assets* are things of value that the entity owns. Examples include cash, investments, and office furniture. *Liabilities* are things the entity owes, its debts. An automobile loan, bank line of credit, and mortgage are all good examples of liabilities. The ability to identify assets and liabilities is an important—and relatively easy—skill to acquire.

In precise financial terms, an organization's assets minus its liabilities equals its net worth. Net worth may be thought of as the monetary value of the organization if all of the liabilities were paid.

For a nonprofit organization, *equity*, or net worth, typically appears on the financial statements as fund balance. Net assets is a somewhat newer term that today's nonprofits use for fund balance. Be prepared to see all four of these terms used interchangeably; they all describe the same thing.

The Accounting Equation

The equity, or net worth (or any of the other names referring to the residual value of an organization), of an organization can always be calculated by subtracting the organization's liabilities from its assets:

$$Equity = Assets - Liabilities$$

As with any numerical equation, there are a number of ways of expressing the same basic formula. When the equation is rewritten as follows, it is a shorthand description of the financial statement known as the balance sheet.

$$Assets = Liabilities + Equity$$

This restatement of the equation is called the accounting equation and can be thought of as a balancing act where one side (assets) cannot exceed, or be exceeded by, the other (liabilities + equity). As you will see, this balancing concept permeates every step of the accounting process.

The balance sheet may be depicted as shown in Figure C-1.

List of Assets	List of Liabilities
1	1
2	2
3	3
4	_____
5	Total Liabilities
6	
7+	
8	
9	Fund Balance
_____ =	_____
$ Total Assets	$ Total Liabilities + Fund Balance

Figure C–1 Balance Sheet

This is the basic framework for a balance sheet. Various other terms—such as equity or net assets—might be substituted for fund balance, but this basic framework remains the same for every balance sheet for every organization—both for-profit and nonprofit. The ordering of assets and liabilities within this framework is also prescribed. The assets should be listed in the order of liquidity. Cash is the most liquid asset, so it is always listed first. The rest of the assets are organized so those that are like cash, or will be turned into cash quickly, are listed before those that are less liquid. Liabilities are listed in the order of maturity, where the first due to be paid off are listed first, followed by those that will be paid in the more distant future.

Revenue and Expense: The Other Two Categories

Revenue, frequently called income, is what the organization earns. Examples of revenue include contributions and similar direct public support, program service revenue, grant revenue, interest and dividend income, and rental income. Remember that, except in the case of contributions, the organization has to earn the money if a cash receipt is to qualify as revenue. Thus, any money received from borrowing does not count as revenue.

Expenses are amounts that are paid for labor, goods, and services so that the organization can continue to provide its own services and produce its own products. Examples of expenses include rent, salaries, and payments for utilities.

Expenses are used-up assets. Cash (one type of asset) becomes an expense when the economic benefits from spending it are used up within the accounting year. Sometimes, an organization spends cash to purchase assets that will help the organization to earn income over a number of years. Such purchases, provided they are significantly large in amount, are referred to as capital items and are capitalized rather than expensed. Some organizations have a policy that all expenditures above a certain amount (e.g.,

$1,000) are to be capitalized. Such capital expenditures take many forms, one of which is the purchase of fixed assets. Fixed assets consist of major property and equipment that the organization expects to own and use for a period of more than one year. The purchase of a building or a photo-copier, for example, is recorded as the purchase of a fixed asset.

Under the generally accepted accounting principle (GAAP) requiring the matching of income with the ex-penses of producing that income (and a related principle, the cost recovery principle), a portion of a fixed capitalized cost is treated as an expense in every year based on the number of years it is estimated that the asset will help the organization to generate revenue.

THE STATEMENT OF REVENUE AND EXPENSES: GETTING TO THE BOTTOM LINE

The statement of revenue and expenses, also called the statement of activities, is the financial reporting document that shows all of the various sources of revenue, or income (individual and totaled), and all of the expenses (individual and totaled), with the difference between the two totals as the bottom line.

Total Revenue – Total Expenses = Excess of Revenue

OVER EXPENSES (THE BOTTOM LINE)

In order for an organization to have a positive bottom line, revenues must exceed expenses. In the business world, this excess is called net income, or profit. When expenses exceed revenue, the bottom line is negative, which repre-sents a loss. A positive bottom line adds to the equity, or net worth, of the organization, whereas a negative bottom line subtracts from it. Because of this cumulative impact on the organization's equity, the bottom line is a major link between the income statement and the balance sheet.

DEBITS AND CREDITS: ANOTHER BALANCING ACT

In considering how an organization's chart of accounts is put together, these questions arise: What goes into and out of each account? How are accounting data summarized most effectively, especially in light of the volume of raw financial data that passes through the organization on any given day? To properly answer these questions, enter the world of double-entry bookkeeping, a place where debits and credits rule—and everything balances.

The methods of double-entry bookkeeping, first described in the 15th century, are so useful—and so elegantly simple—that they continue in use to this day. The double-entry system used by accountants today continues to record every transaction on two sides (debits and credits), with one side of the transaction always balancing with the other. So, at any given time, if "everything balances," the accountant can be sure that every accounting entry is complete.

Cash Basis Accounting

The cash basis method is typically used by smaller organizations. Under this arrangement, transactions are only recorded when cash "moves." Income is earned when the money is received; expenses are counted when the money is spent. Under this approach, all the receipts and payments entered into the organization's checkbook in a particular period are summarized in the financial statements for that particular period. (An accounting period can be any part of either a calendar year or a fiscal year. A financial year ending on December 31 is referred to as a calendar year; a financial year ending on any date other than December 31 is referred to as a fiscal year.)

Cash basis statements are filled with useful information. Statement users can learn a lot about the organization's financial activities and position from them. However, be aware of distortions that can occur. Cash basis statements have a way of masking economic reality. This result can be intentional or unintentional. In either event, it creates problems for statement readers.

For example, under the cash basis, the organization's financial picture can be improved simply by leaving some of the bills unpaid or accelerating collections for services or dues at the end of the year. Similarly, favorable financial results can be played down by paying every bill and taking a more casual approach to collections. In such situations, important and useful information is being left out, and the financial statements are incomplete when the cash basis is used. Unless the statement user is aware that important information is missing, the statements can be quite misleading.

Accrual Basis Accounting

In some situations, cash basis income may actually approximate accrual basis income. However, cash basis financial statements will not conform to economic reality when significant noncash transactions are left out of the financial statements. Bringing these noncash transactions into the financial statements—to more accurately reflect economic reality—is what accrual basis accounting is all about.

Like the cash method, the accrual method begins with a summary of all of the cash activity for a particular accounting period. But it does not end there. The financial records are then adjusted to reflect economic activity outside of the cash account.

Accrual accounting attempts to sort financial data into a time period in which it really belongs. The resulting financial statements are generally more useful than financial statements that are prepared on a cash basis.

The accounting profession has given accrual accounting its official stamp of approval. In fact, financial statements must be prepared on an accrual basis to conform to GAAP. Accrual accounting and the matching principle of GAAP go hand in hand by requiring that income, and expense incurred in creating that income, be recognized in the same period.

The use of accrual basis accounting has spawned some interesting terms that identify and describe noncash accounts.

- *Accounts receivable*—An asset account, this represents cash still due to the organization when it sells a product or service to an outside entity that agrees to pay later.

- *Prepaid expenses*—An asset account, this represents amounts the organization has paid currently for an item or service that will be used in the future. Prepaid insurance and prepaid rent are examples of prepaid expenses. Under the cash basis, such amounts would appear on the financial statements as expenses instead of assets, even though future economic benefit is to be derived from them.

- *Accounts payable*—A liability account, this represents the amount of cash the organization still owes when it incurs a cost or buys an item now but will pay later. Unpaid bills for office supplies and utilities are examples of accounts payable.

- *Unearned revenue*—A liability account, this is sometimes referred to as deferred revenue. It represents payments that the organization receives in advance for goods or services to be provided in the future. Unearned member dues are a good example of cash receipts that should be recorded as a liability. At the end of the current year, the organization receives dues for the following year; services for that income has not yet been earned. By recording these cash receipts as a liability in the period in which they are received, they can later appear as revenues in the period in which the income is actually earned.

Budgeting Issues: A Primer for Nonprofit Executive Directors

M y father is not a good example on this issue. He took the position that budgeting, although it did influence prudence, stood in the way of too many of his pleasures in life. On the other hand, my oddball cousin Julian was a stickler for budgeting, and he'd do it on a weekly basis. It was the 1920s and he worked for the Army Air Corps at Mitchell Field, Long Island. He was a "doper," meaning that he applied highly odorous dope (no ventilation systems then) to the canvas fabric that then covered the wings and fuselages of the aircraft all day long, day in and day out. Coincidentally, he meandered through life with a perpetual, beatific, dope-induced smile.

Each week, Julian would collect his paycheck, cash it, give his mother (he lived with his parents) the usual $12 stipend, put $7 to $10 in his left pocket for weekend food, lodging, cigarettes, and miscellaneous expenses, and put the balance in his right pocket. Then he'd go to the Greyhound bus station, hand the ticket man whatever was in his right pocket, and buy a round-trip ticket to the farthest point that the balance would take him. I recommend it.

In order to properly account for the funds at a non-profit, the organization must have a budget. The board and staff usually collaborate on developing the figures included in the budget document. But the ED has to live with that document, making sure the organization meets everything that is laid out in it. If the ED is unable to follow the budget, the board is certain to ask why.

PUTTING THE BUDGET TOGETHER

A well-prepared budget is the organization's blueprint for action. It is the planning document that expresses the organization's objectives in the most specific, concrete terms possible. Developing the budget figures involves the following steps:

1. ***Determine the cost of each objective.*** Do not underestimate the difficulty of doing this task. Begin by gathering all direct costs (those specific to a given cost objective or program). The next step is to apply indirect costs (those not traceable to a specific program, such as administrative costs) on a reasonable and consistent basis. The very first time this is done, refer to a cost accounting text or get help from a staff member or volunteer in the organization who is reasonably well-versed in the challenges of cost accounting.

2. ***Determine available revenues.*** Once it is known how much the nonprofit is planning to spend, identify the sources of revenues. Will the project be self-funded or funded primarily by outside grants? Are there general revenues, such as unrestricted support, that can be used? The amount of projected revenues should be based on what the nonprofit actually expects to receive during the

---

Source: Reprinted from A.S. Lang, *A Practical Guide in Nonprofit Financial Management,* © 1995, Aspen Publishers, Inc.

budget period. Even when this amount is based on last year's numbers, be sure to consider the various factors that might change this amount during the budget period. This step can be very challenging and time-consuming and requires a combination of good judgement and imagination. Get input from as many sources as possible in the time available.

3. *Compare estimated costs to estimated revenues.* This step allows for a determination of the comparative profitability of various activities. It also allows the nonprofit to see how each program will contribute or consume overall organizational income.

4. *Develop the final plan.* Once all of the data have been organized, the time has arrived for hammering out the final plan. Someone usually has to make some tough decisions at this time. If the total budget projects a deficit, certain programs or activities may have to be trimmed or eliminated. Alternatively, the organization may decide to tap its reserves. If the budget projects a substantial profit, budgeting for additional expenditures may be warranted. Remember, every phase of the budgeting process takes time. There are always wrinkles to be ironed out, and sometimes major changes are required. The process will work best when such adjustments are made by the individual responsible for managing that portion of the budget.

UNDERSTANDING RESERVES

In challenging economic times, reserves can be the difference between success and failure for a nonprofit organization.

Source: Reprinted from A.S. Lang, "Reserves: A Primer," *Nonprofit Financial Advisor*, Vol. 12, © 1994, Aspen Publishers, Inc.

When revenues dwindle and borrowing becomes difficult, reserves help a nonprofit finance continuing operations.

Different people define reserves in different ways. Many nonprofits use a classic definition: total assets (what is owed) less total liabilities (what is owed). Unfortunately, this definition has severe limitations: It includes assets (such as buildings and equipment) that cannot be used to pay operating expenses; similarly, it includes liabilities (long-term debt) for which the need for payment will arise only in later years. A more conservative and useful definition of reserves is current, liquid assets (cash and assets that can be readily converted into cash) less current liabilities.

Nonprofits usually express reserves as a percentage of one year's total operating expenses. Thus, an association with a reserve of 100 percent would have reserves equal to one year's operating expenses. A reserve of 100 percent is ideal—and very rare. The industry averages about 40 percent. Larger associations tend to have a smaller percentage of reserves because the higher absolute dollar amount of their reserves compensates for the lower percentage. Endowments have the highest levels of reserves because they can spend only income (and not the endowment itself).

It is possible, but extremely unusual, for an organization to have excessive reserves. Political problems can arise if contributors see an organization building up reserves year after year to a point that is greatly in excess of what the organization could reasonably need. Reserves in excess of a full year's operating expenses will usually cause raised eyebrows and tough questions from contributors. In fact, some public charity watchdog groups have begun to monitor reserve levels and report what they consider to be excessive reserves to the public. In extreme cases, excessive reserves can also cause problems with the Internal Revenue Service (IRS). But in most cases, contributors will object long before reserves reach a level that would cause problems with the IRS.

Think about building reserves in good times, so that the nonprofit can have them in bad times. Most charities do not like to think about building reserves; if they have extra money, they prefer to use it on program services to further their charitable purposes. On the other hand, consider that by forgoing a modest expansion of services today, the nonprofit may be able to avoid a major retrenchment tomorrow.

If the reserves are currently too low, consider adding reserve building as a budget item. Putting reserves on the budget ensures that they will be seriously reconsidered on a regular basis and commits the organization to specific targets. As reserves approach their target level, the amount budgeted can be decreased.

Index